LEARNINGEXPRESS BASIC SKILLS FOR COLLEGE

WRITING SKILLS

FOR COLLEGE STUDENTS

Judith F. Olson

Prentice Hall

Library of Congress Cataloging-in-Publication Data

Olson, Judith F.

    Writing skills for college students / Judith F. Olson.

       p.   cm. — (LearningExpress basic skills for college)

    ISBN 0-13-080256-5

     1. English language—Rhetoric—Problems, exercises, etc. 2. English language—Grammar—Problems, exercises, etc. 3. Academic writing—Problems, exercises, etc. I. Title. II. Series.

  PE1413.047   1997

  808′.042—dc21

                                                                                              97-43620
                                                                                             CIP

Acquisitions Editor: *Todd Rossell*
Managing Editor: *Mary Carnis*
Director of Manufacturing & Production: *Bruce Johnson*
Manufacturing Buyer: *Marc Bove*
Editorial Assistant: *Amy Diehl*

© 1998 by LearningExpress, LLC.
Published by Prentice Hall, Inc.
Simon & Schuster/A Viacom Company
Upper Saddle River, New Jersey 07458

Printed in the United States of America

10 9 8 7 6 5 4 3 2 1

ISBN 0-13-080256-5

Prentice Hall International (UK) Limited, *London*
Prentice Hall of Australia Pty. Limited, *Sydney*
Prentice Hall of Canada Inc., *Toronto*
Prentice Hall Hispanoamericana, S.A., *Mexico*
Prentice Hall of India Private Limited, *New Delhi*
Prentice Hall of Japan, Inc., *Tokyo*
Simon & Schuster Asia Pte. Ltd., *Singapore*
Editora Prentice Hall do Brasil, Ltda., *Rio de Janeiro*

OTHER TITLES FROM PRENTICE HALL

ACKNOWLEDGEMENTS

We would like to thank the following people for reviewing the Basic Skills for College series. These books are better as a result of their time and effort:

Jerry Bouchie, St. Cloud State University
Kathy Carpenter, Ph.D., University of Nebraska at Kearney
Dr. Thomas R. Gier, University of Alaska, Anchorage
Karen R. Olson, University of New Mexico
Celesia Snyder, Ohio State University, Newark/Central Ohio Technical College

Very special thanks for their efforts go to Jan Gallagher, James Gish, and Barry Lippman at LearningExpress. Their efforts and those of their staff were essential and invaluable in making this series successful.

We appreciate the hours of diligent work of those at Prentice Hall: Mary Carnis, Marc Bove, Santos Shih, Rit Dojny, Irene Hess, Dave Jagger, Julio Cassanelli, Bryon Smith, Clarence Diehl, Sue Bierman, Juanita Griffin, Katie Bradford, Frank Mortimer, Christopher Eastman, Todd Rossell, and especially to Amy Diehl for her tireless hours of service.

LearningExpress Basic Skills for College

Introducing a new series that helps build basic skills *fast!* Each book offers essential tips and techniques plus plenty of practice exercises in critical skill areas. Ideal for individuals preparing for their first year of college. A must for those who need to polish the skills that lead to success.

Math Skills for College Students (ISBN 0-13-080257-3)
Reading Skills for College Students (ISBN 0-13-080258-1)
Vocabulary & Spelling Skills for
College Students (ISBN 0-13-080255-7)
Writing Skills for College Students (ISBN 0-13-080256-5)

CONTENTS

INTRODUCTION

Writing is a lot like fishing. People who are good at fishing study and practice it. They learn which tools to use for catching the best fish in different types of water. No one is born with fishing talent. Some people enjoy it more than others, but everyone can do it if they want. The same goes for writing.

Since you bought this book, you probably want or need to learn more about the process of writing and how to become a better writer. If you complete each lesson in this book, you can acquire the mysterious and coveted power of the pen. This book covers the basics of writing: punctuation, usage, diction, and organization. These are vital skills that will help you to write better in all your college courses. You'll find no fluff in this book; it's for busy students who want to learn as much as they can as efficiently as possible. Each lesson contains enough illustrations for you to get the idea, opportunities to practice the skills, and suggestions for using them in your daily life.

Many students fear a blank sheet of paper or an empty computer screen. "I just don't know what to write. Even when I know what I want to say, I'm afraid it will come out looking wrong or sounding stupid."

But that's one of the things to love about writing. Writing is a process. The first time you write a draft, it doesn't matter if your writing comes out wrong or sounds stupid because you can change it as often as you want. You can go over until you're completely satisfied, or until you need to shift gears and study another subject. You can show your draft to your roommates, friends, or family—people who are used to hearing you sound stupid—and get a response before you ever hand it in to your instructor.

Don't put pressure on yourself by thinking you need to write a perfect first draft for any of your assignments. No one can sit down and write out polished essays, reports, or stories without changing (or revising) them at least a little bit. Even the pros have to revise their work. For instance, the writer Ernest Hemingway had to revise the last page of his famous novel *A Farewell to Arms* thirty-nine times before he was satisfied with it. You probably won't want to revise an essay that many times before handing it in to your instructor, but even if you write two or three drafts of an assignment, you certainly aren't alone in your need for revision.

Writing has three distinct advantages over speaking:

1. In writing, you can take it back. The spoken word, however, cannot be revised. Once you make a statement verbally, it affects your listeners in a particular way and you can't "take it back" or rephrase it to the point that the first statement is forgotten. However, if you write a statement down and, after looking at it, realize that it sounds offensive or incorrect, you can revise it before giving it to the intended audience. Writing is a careful, thoughtful way of communicating.

2. Writing forces you to clarify your thoughts. If you're having trouble writing, it's often because you're not yet finished with the thinking part. Sometimes just sitting down and writing whatever is on your mind helps you discover and organize what you think.

3. Another advantage is permanence. Ideas presented in writing carry far more weight than spoken ideas. Additionally, they can be reviewed and referred to in their exact, original form. Spoken ideas rely upon the sometimes inaccurate memories of other people.

Writing is nothing more than thought on paper—considered, organized thought. Many people are protective of their thoughts and, therefore, prefer to keep them hidden inside their heads. Some thoughts should be kept private, perhaps, but many great ideas and observations are never born because their creators won't express them. This book can help you express your ideas in a clear and grammatically correct way. After you learn how to insert commas and semicolons correctly, use verbs to create strong images in your writing, and the other basic skills taught in this book, you'll gain confidence in your writing ability. In fact, you'll be able to move forward and master more complex writing concerns after you get the basics down. You'll be required to do a lot of writing throughout your college career, so the skills you learn in this book will be put to good use.

The lessons in this book are designed to be completed in about 20 minutes apiece. If you do a lesson every weekday, you can finish the whole course is about a month. However, you may find another approach that works better for you. You'll find you make more progress, though, if you complete at least two lessons a week. If you leave too much time between lessons, you'll forget what you've learned.

By the time you finish this book, you will not only possess better writing skills, but you'll probably also have better critical thinking skills as well because writing and thinking are so closely related. Many college courses, ranging from composition to history to psychology, share the goal of increasing students' critical thinking skills. So you'll have a head start in your other courses with the new critical thinking skills you've developed. If you practice in class what you've learned in this book, it won't take long for your instructors to notice the new and improved you. That's what practice does—it helps you get better at whatever it is you're spending time doing, whether it's fishing or writing. So dive into the first lesson of this book and get ready to improve your writing skills. Good luck!

WRITING SKILLS PRETEST

Before you start your study of grammar and writing skills, you may want to get an idea of how much you already know and how much you need to learn. If that's the case, take the pretest that follows.

The pretest is 50 multiple-choice questions covering all the lessons in this book. Naturally, 50 questions can't cover every single concept or rule you will learn by working through this book. So even if you get all of the questions on the pretest right, it's almost guaranteed that you will find a few ideas or rules in this book that you didn't already know. On the other hand, if you get a lot of the answers wrong on this pretest, don't despair. This book will show you how to get better at grammar and writing, step by step.

So use this pretest just to get a general idea of how much of what's in this book you already know. If you get a high score on this pretest, you may be able to spend less time with this book than you originally planned. If you get a low score, you may find that you will need more than 20 minutes a day to get through each chapter and learn all the grammar and mechanics concepts you need.

There's an answer sheet you can use for filling in the correct answers on the next page. Or, if you prefer, simply circle the answer numbers in this book. If the book doesn't belong to you, write the numbers 1–50 on a piece of paper and record your answers there. Take as much time as you need to do this short test. When you finish, check your answers against the answer key that follows this test. Each answer tells you which lesson of this book teaches you about the grammatical rule in that question.

1.	ⓐ	ⓑ	ⓒ	ⓓ
2.	ⓐ	ⓑ	ⓒ	ⓓ
3.	ⓐ	ⓑ	ⓒ	ⓓ
4.	ⓐ	ⓑ	ⓒ	ⓓ
5.	ⓐ	ⓑ	ⓒ	ⓓ
6.	ⓐ	ⓑ	ⓒ	ⓓ
7.	ⓐ	ⓑ	ⓒ	ⓓ
8.	ⓐ	ⓑ	ⓒ	ⓓ
9.	ⓐ	ⓑ	ⓒ	ⓓ
10.	ⓐ	ⓑ	ⓒ	ⓓ
11.	ⓐ	ⓑ	ⓒ	ⓓ
12.	ⓐ	ⓑ	ⓒ	ⓓ
13.	ⓐ	ⓑ	ⓒ	ⓓ
14.	ⓐ	ⓑ	ⓒ	ⓓ
15.	ⓐ	ⓑ	ⓒ	ⓓ
16.	ⓐ	ⓑ	ⓒ	ⓓ
17.	ⓐ	ⓑ	ⓒ	ⓓ
18.	ⓐ	ⓑ	ⓒ	ⓓ
19.	ⓐ	ⓑ	ⓒ	ⓓ
20.	ⓐ	ⓑ	ⓒ	ⓓ
21.	ⓐ	ⓑ	ⓒ	ⓓ
22.	ⓐ	ⓑ	ⓒ	ⓓ
23.	ⓐ	ⓑ	ⓒ	ⓓ
24.	ⓐ	ⓑ	ⓒ	ⓓ
25.	ⓐ	ⓑ	ⓒ	ⓓ
26.	ⓐ	ⓑ	ⓒ	ⓓ
27.	ⓐ	ⓑ	ⓒ	ⓓ
28.	ⓐ	ⓑ	ⓒ	ⓓ
29.	ⓐ	ⓑ	ⓒ	ⓓ
30.	ⓐ	ⓑ	ⓒ	ⓓ
31.	ⓐ	ⓑ	ⓒ	ⓓ
32.	ⓐ	ⓑ	ⓒ	ⓓ
33.	ⓐ	ⓑ	ⓒ	ⓓ
34.	ⓐ	ⓑ	ⓒ	ⓓ
35.	ⓐ	ⓑ	ⓒ	ⓓ
36.	ⓐ	ⓑ	ⓒ	ⓓ
37.	ⓐ	ⓑ	ⓒ	ⓓ
38.	ⓐ	ⓑ	ⓒ	ⓓ
39.	ⓐ	ⓑ	ⓒ	ⓓ
40.	ⓐ	ⓑ	ⓒ	ⓓ
41.	ⓐ	ⓑ	ⓒ	ⓓ
42.	ⓐ	ⓑ	ⓒ	ⓓ
43.	ⓐ	ⓑ	ⓒ	ⓓ
44.	ⓐ	ⓑ	ⓒ	ⓓ
45.	ⓐ	ⓑ	ⓒ	ⓓ
46.	ⓐ	ⓑ	ⓒ	ⓓ
47.	ⓐ	ⓑ	ⓒ	ⓓ
48.	ⓐ	ⓑ	ⓒ	ⓓ
49.	ⓐ	ⓑ	ⓒ	ⓓ
50.	ⓐ	ⓑ	ⓒ	ⓓ

PRETEST

1. Which version of the sentence is correctly capitalized?
   a. Last Thursday, my Mother, my Aunt Sarah, and I went to the museum to see an exhibit of African art.
   b. Last Thursday, my mother, my Aunt Sarah, and I went to the museum to see an exhibit of African art.
   c. Last Thursday, my mother, my aunt Sarah, and I went to the Museum to see an exhibit of African art.
   d. Last thursday, my mother, my aunt Sarah, and I went to the museum to see an exhibit of African Art.

2. Which of the underlined words in the following sentence should be capitalized?

   The <u>governor</u> gave a speech at the <u>fourth</u> of July picnic, which was held at my <u>cousin's</u> farm five miles <u>east</u> of town.

   a. governor
   b. fourth
   c. cousin's
   d. east

3. Which of the underlined words in the following sentence should be capitalized?

   "Last <u>semester</u>, I wrote my <u>history</u> report on the Korean <u>war</u>," my <u>sister</u> told me.

   a. semester
   b. history
   c. war
   d. sister

4. Which version uses periods correctly?
   a. Dr Harrison will speak at a hotel in Chicago, Ill, on Thurs at 3:00 P.M.
   b. Dr. Harrison will speak at a hotel in Chicago, Ill, on Thurs at 3:00 PM.
   c. Dr Harrison will speak at a hotel in Chicago, Ill, on Thurs. at 3:00 P.M.
   d. Dr. Harrison will speak at a hotel in Chicago, Ill., on Thurs. at 3:00 P.M.

5. Which version uses punctuation correctly?
   a. Watch out. The road is icy?
   b. Watch out! The road is icy.
   c. Watch out? The road is icy!
   d. Watch out, the road is icy?

6. Which one is a sentence fragment, that is, NOT a complete sentence?
   a. Hearing the thunder, the lifeguard ordered us out of the water.
   b. Turn off the lights.
   c. Sunday afternoon spent reading and playing computer games.
   d. I was surprised to see that my neighbor had written a letter to the editor.

7. Three of the following sentences are faulty. They are either run-ons or comma splices. Which one is NOT a faulty sentence?
   a. The newspapers are supposed to be delivered by 7:00, but I am usually finished before 6:45.
   b. I called the delivery service this morning, they told me the shipment would arrive on time.
   c. Look in the closet you should find it there.
   d. I was the first to sign the petition Harry was second.

8. Which version is punctuated correctly?
   a. Charlotte, who ran in the Boston Marathon last year will compete in this year's New York Marathon.
   b. Charlotte who ran in the Boston Marathon, last year, will compete in this year's New York Marathon.
   c. Charlotte who ran in the Boston Marathon last year, will compete in this year's New York Marathon.
   d. Charlotte, who ran in the Boston Marathon last year, will compete in this year's New York Marathon.

9. Which version is punctuated correctly?
   a. The park service will not allow anyone, who does not have a camping permit, to use this campground.
   b. The park service will not allow anyone who does not have a camping permit to use this campground.
   c. The park service will not allow anyone, who does not have a camping permit to use this campground.
   d. The park service will not allow anyone who does not have a camping permit, to use this campground.

10. Which version is punctuated correctly?
    a. As soon as he finished his homework, Rod, who is a member of the baseball team, went to batting practice.
    b. As soon as he finished his homework Rod, who is a member of the baseball team went to batting practice.
    c. As soon as he finished, his homework, Rod who is a member of the baseball team, went to batting practice.
    d. As soon as he finished his homework, Rod who is a member of the baseball team went to batting practice.

11. Which of the underlined portions of the sentence below is punctuated INCORRECTLY?

    My mother was born on (a) <u>December 15, 1944,</u> in Kingwood, West (b) <u>Virginia, when</u> she was (c) <u>five, her</u> family moved to (d) <u>347 Benton Street, Zanesville, Ohio.</u>

12. Which version is punctuated correctly?
    a. Yes I would like to see a copy of the report and please send it today by priority mail.
    b. Yes, I would like to see a copy of the report and please send it, today by priority mail.
    c. Yes, I would like to see a copy of the report and, please send it today by priority mail.
    d. Yes, I would like to see a copy of the report, and please send it today by priority mail.

13. Which version is punctuated correctly?
    a. I'm sorry, Bart, that you cannot meet us for dinner tonight. We'll phone you again next Friday.
    b. I'm sorry, Bart that you cannot meet us for dinner tonight. We'll phone you again next Friday.
    c. I'm sorry Bart that you cannot meet us for dinner tonight. We'll phone you again next Friday.
    d. I'm sorry, Bart, that you cannot meet us for dinner tonight, we'll phone you again next Friday.

14. Which is the correct punctuation for the underlined portion?

The weather forecasters are predicting ten inches of snow <u>tonight therefore</u> the annual chili supper will be rescheduled for next week.

a. tonight, therefore
b. tonight, therefore,
c. tonight; therefore,
d. tonight, therefore;

15. Which is the correct punctuation for the underlined portion?

You may choose to read any two of the following <u>novels *The*</u> Great Gatsby, *Song of Solomon, Sophie's Choice, The Color Purple, The Bell Jar,* and *The Invisible Man.*

a. novels, *The*
b. novels: *The*
c. novels; *the*
d. novels. *The*

16. Which version is punctuated correctly?
a. One of my concerns—if you really want to know is that the city council will vote against the new plan.
b. One of my concerns—if you really want to know—is that the city council will vote against the new plan.
c. One of my concerns, if you really want to know—is that the city council will vote against the new plan.
d. One of my concerns if you really want to know is that the city council will vote against the new plan.

17. Which version is punctuated correctly?
a. You will find boys' shirts in the childrens' department.
b. You will find boy's shirts in the children's department.
c. You will find boys' shirts in the children's department.
d. You will find boy's shirts in the childrens' department.

18. Which version is punctuated correctly?
a. Whose coat is this? Is it yours or Eric's?
b. Whose coat is this? Is it your's or Eric's?
c. Who's coat is this? Is it your's or Eric's?
d. Who's coat is this? Is it yours or Eric's?

19. Which version is punctuated correctly?
a. "May I ride with you?" asked Del. "I can't get my car started."
b. May I ride with you? asked Del. "I can't get my car started."
c. "May I ride with you? asked Del. I can't get my car started."
d. "May I ride with you"? asked Del, "I can't get my car started."

20. Which of the following should be placed in quotation marks and should NOT be italicized or underlined?
a. the name of a ship
b. the title of a poem
c. the title of a novel
d. the name of a newspaper

21. Which version uses hyphens correctly?
  a. The well-known singer-songwriter gave a three hour concert.
  b. The well known singer songwriter gave a three-hour concert.
  c. The well-known singer-songwriter gave a three-hour concert.
  d. The well known singer-songwriter gave a three hour concert.

22. Which of the following should NOT be hyphenated?
  a. twenty-one students
  b. two-inch nails
  c. a thirty-minute interview
  d. ten-feet of rope

23. Which version uses parentheses correctly?
  a. I plan to do my geography report on the Central American country of Belize (formerly known as British Honduras).
  b. I plan to do my geography report on the (Central American country of) Belize, formerly known as British Honduras.
  c. I plan to do my (geography) report on the Central American country of Belize, formerly known as British Honduras.
  d. I plan to do my geography report on the Central American country (of Belize) formerly known as British Honduras.

For questions 24 and 25, choose the correct verb form.

24. Last night, Rita _____ a standing ovation for her performance.
  a. has gotten
  b. gotten
  c. will get
  d. got

25. Bart _____ cupcakes so we could all celebrate his birthday.
  a. brang
  b. brought
  c. bring
  d. had brung

26. Which of the following underlined verbs is NOT written in the correct tense?

Last week, we (a) <u>went</u> camping in Zion National Park. We (b) <u>hike</u> several hours each day. At night, I (c) <u>climbed</u> into my sleeping bag exhausted, but in the morning I (d) <u>couldn't wait</u> to get started again.

27. Choose the version that correctly rewrites the following sentence in the active voice.

I was taken to the public library by my sister before I was able to read.
  a. Before I was able to read, I was taken to the public library by my sister.
  b. Before learning to read, my sister took me to the public library.
  c. Before I was able to read, my sister took me to the public library.
  d. I was taken to the public library before I knew how to read, by my sister.

28. Which of the following sentences is in the passive voice?
  a. On Saturday nights, we made popcorn.
  b. Our bowls were filled and brought into the living room.
  c. We sat on the floor and watched the movie we had rented.
  d. One of us usually fell asleep before the movie was over.

For questions 29 and 30, choose the verb that agrees with the subject of the sentence.

29. Neither of the dogs _____ to obedience training.
    a. have been
    b. were
    c. is been
    d. has been

30. The art professor, along with several of her students, _____ to attend the gallery opening tomorrow evening.
    a. is planning
    b. are planning
    c. plan
    d. have planned

31. Choose the subject that agrees with the verb in the following sentence.

    _____ of the customers have complained about poor service.

    a. One
    b. Neither
    c. Each
    d. Some

32. In which of the following sentences is the underlined verb NOT in agreement with the subject of the sentence?

    a. Where <u>are</u> the forms you want me to fill out?
    b. Which <u>is</u> the correct form?
    c. Here <u>is</u> the forms you need to complete.
    d. There <u>are</u> two people who still need to complete the form.

33. In which of the following sentences is the underlined pronoun INCORRECT?
    a. Alicia and <u>me</u> want to spend Saturday at Six Flags Amusement Park.
    b. Either Sam or William will bring <u>his</u> CD player to the party.
    c. She and <u>I</u> will work together on the project.
    d. Why won't you let <u>her</u> come with us?

34. In which of the following sentences is the underlined pronoun INCORRECT?
    a. Francine can run much faster than <u>me.</u>
    b. Erin and Bob are painting the house <u>themselves.</u>
    c. Five members of the team and <u>I</u> will represent our school.
    d. Our neighbors gave <u>us</u> some tomatoes from their garden.

For questions 35–38, choose the option that correctly completes the sentence.

35. Four band members and _____ were chosen to attend the state competition. One of _____ will do the driving.
    a. me, we
    b. me, us
    c. I, we
    d. I, us

36. Marcus _____ the bags of groceries on the kitchen table fifteen minutes ago.
    a. had sat
    b. set
    c. sit
    d. sat

37. About five minutes after the sun _____, my alarm goes off, and _____ time to get up.
a. raises, it's
b. raises, its
c. rises, it's
d. rises, its

38. Paula did _____ on the test, but Georgia had the _____ score in the class.
a. good, better
b. good, best
c. well, better
d. well, best

39. Which of the sentences is clearly and correctly written?
a. Driving along the country road, a deer ran in front of us.
b. A deer ran in front of us while driving along the country road.
c. As we were driving along the country road, a deer ran in front of us.
d. Running in front of us, we saw the deer, driving along the country road.

For questions 40–46, choose the option that correctly completes the sentence.

40. If we divide this pizza _____ the five people here, there won't be _____ pieces left over.
a. among, any
b. among, no
c. between, any
d. between, no

41. Yesterday, I _____ the campers to the _____ we had chosen near the river.
a. lead, cite
b. lead, site
c. led, cite
d. led, site

42. As we have done in the _____, we will _____ at the coffee house at 10:00 A.M.
a. past, meet
b. past, meat
c. passed, meet
d. passed, meat

43. As you can _____ see, there has been a _____ in the water pipe.
a. planely, brake
b. planely, break
c. plainly, brake
d. plainly, break

44. Do you know _____ Teresa will _____ to join our organization?
a. weather, choose
b. weather, chose
c. whether, choose
d. whether, chose

45. _____ are the magazines that _____ to be stacked on this table?
a. Wear, used
b. Wear, use
c. Where, used
d. Where, use

46. Do you _____ if the Giants _____ the game?
   a. know, one
   b. know, won
   c. no, one
   d. no, won

47. Which of the following phrases contains a redundancy; that is, it repeats words that express the same idea?
   a. I did not hear the phone ring.
   b. You always perform your job efficiently.
   c. The umpire has temporarily suspended the game until later.
   d. Jenna and Erin have both contributed greatly to our team's success.

48. Which of the following sentences contains a cliché?
   a. The room was so quiet, you could hear a pin drop.
   b. Your plan is not in accordance with the regulations set down by the review board.
   c. The stars were pinpricks in the tarpaper sky.
   d. Due to the fact that it snowed, the trip was canceled.

49. Which version has a consistent point of view?
   a. The history of English is divided into three periods. You could mark the earliest one at about the fifth century A.D.
   b. You can say that the history of English could be divided into three periods, and I know the earliest one begins about the fifth century A.D.
   c. The history of English is divided into three periods. The earliest one begins at about the fifth century A.D.
   d. I learned that the history of English is divided into three periods and that you begin the earliest one at about the fifth century A.D.

50. Which version has a parallel structure?
   a. We write for a variety of purposes: in expressing our feelings, to convey information, to persuade, or to give pleasure.
   b. We write for a variety of purposes: to express our feelings, convey information, persuasion, or giving pleasure.
   c. We write for a variety of purposes: an expression of our feelings, conveying information, persuade, or to give pleasure.
   d. We write for a variety of purposes: to express our feelings, to convey information, to persuade, or to give pleasure.

ANSWER KEY

If you miss any of the answers, you can find help for that kind of question in the lesson shown to the right of the answer.

1. b. Lesson 1
2. b. Lesson 1
3. c. Lesson 1
4. d. Lesson 2
5. b. Lesson 2
6. c. Lesson 3
7. a. Lesson 3
8. d. Lesson 4
9. b. Lesson 4
10. a. Lesson 4
11. b. Lessons 5, 6
12. d. Lesson 5
13. a. Lesson 5
14. c. Lesson 6
15. b. Lesson 6
16. b. Lesson 7
17. c. Lesson 7
18. a. Lesson 7
19. a. Lesson 8
20. b. Lesson 8
21. c. Lesson 9
22. d. Lesson 9
23. a. Lesson 9
24. d. Lesson 10
25. b. Lesson 10

26. b. Lesson 10
27. c. Lesson 11
28. b. Lesson 11
29. d. Lesson 12
30. a. Lesson 12
31. d. Lesson 12
32. c. Lesson 12
33. a. Lesson 13
34. a. Lesson 13
35. d. Lesson 13
36. b. Lesson 14
37. c. Lesson 14
38. d. Lesson 14
39. c. Lesson 15
40. a. Lesson 15
41. d. Lesson 16
42. a. Lesson 16
43. d. Lesson 16
44. c. Lesson 17
45. c. Lesson 17
46. b. Lesson 17
47. c. Lesson 18
48. a. Lesson 18
49. c. Lesson 19
50. d. Lesson 19

L·E·S·S·O·N
CAPITALIZATION
1

LESSON SUMMARY

Today you'll learn about the fine points of capitalization. The chapter divides capitalization rules into two kinds: general rules governing capitalization and specific rules regarding proper nouns and adjectives.

Start by seeing just how much you already know about the proper use of capital letters. On the next page you see the same passage written twice. The first column, called **Problem,** contains no capitalization at all—definitely a problem in writing! Circle those letters you think should be capitalized in the **Problem** column, and then check yourself against the **Solution** column.

Problem

when I first saw the black hills on january 2, 1995, i was shocked by their beauty. we had just spent new year's day in sioux falls, south dakota, and had headed west toward our home in denver, colorado. as we traveled along interstate 90, i could see the black hills rising slightly in the distance. after driving through the badlands and stopping at wall drug in wall, south dakota, the evergreen-covered hills broke the barren monotony of the landscape. my oldest daughter said, "dad, look! there's something that's not all white." we saw mount rushmore and custer state park, the home of the largest herd of buffalo in north america. we also drove the treacherous spearfish canyon road. fortunately, our jeep cherokee had no trouble with the ice and snow on the winding road. we were unable to see needles national park because the needles highway was snowed shut. winter may not be the best time to see these sights, but we enjoyed them nonetheless.

Solution

When I first saw the Black Hills on January 2, 1995, I was shocked by their beauty. We had just spent New Year's Day in Sioux Falls, South Dakota, and had headed west toward our home in Denver, Colorado. As we traveled along Interstate 90, I could see the Black Hills rising slightly in the distance. After driving through the Badlands and stopping at Wall Drug in Wall, South Dakota, the evergreen-covered hills broke the barren monotony of the landscape. My oldest daughter said, "Dad, look! There's something that's not all white." We saw Mount Rushmore and Custer State Park, the home of the largest herd of buffalo in North America. We also drove the treacherous Spearfish Canyon Road. Fortunately, our Jeep Cherokee had no trouble with the ice and snow on the winding road. We were unable to see Needles National Park because the Needles Highway was snowed shut. Winter may not be the best time to see these sights, but we enjoyed them nonetheless.

How did you do? As you progress through the lesson, try to identify the specific rules that you missed.

GENERAL CAPITALIZATION RULES

The table below summarizes general capitalization rules. Rules having to do with specific categories of proper nouns are dealt with in the next section.

CAPITALIZATION RULES

Rule	Example
Capitalize the first word of a sentence. If the first word is a number, write it as a word.	This is the first word of the sentence. Three of us worked the early shift.
Capitalize the pronoun *I* or the contraction *I'm*, and the abbreviations *B.C.* or *A.D.*	The group left when **I** asked them to go. The manuscript was dated 501 **A.D.**
Capitalize the first word of a quotation. Do not capitalize the first word of a partial quotation.	I said, "**W**hat's the name of your dog?" He called me "the worst excuse for a student" he had ever seen.

Below is an example of a dialogue that illustrates the above rules. (A note about paragraphing in dialogue: Each time a speaker finishes, begin a new paragraph.)

"**G**ood morning," said the new supervisor as **I** entered the door.

"**G**ood morning!" **I** answered, somewhat surprised. "**Y**ou must be Ms. Barnes. **I**'m Joshua Haines. **I**t's a pleasure to meet you."

"**T**ell me what you do, Joshua. **I**'m anxious to learn all about this operation."

I smiled and said, "**T**hat doesn't surprise me. **I** heard you were a '**s**ieve for information.'"

PRACTICE

Check your ability to apply the rules above in the practice questions below. Choose the correctly capitalized option from each of the sets below. Answers to each set of questions can be found at the end of the lesson.

1. a. the memo confused me at first. after a few readings i was able to understand it.
 b. The memo confused me at first. after a few readings I was able to understand it.
 c. The memo confused me at first. After a few readings I was able to understand it.

2. a. "where are you going?" my coworker asked.
  "to a meeting i'm not very excited about," i answered.
 b. "Where are you going?" my coworker asked.
  "To a meeting I'm not very excited about," I answered.
 c. "Where are you going?" My coworker asked.
  "To a meeting I'm not very excited about," I answered.

3. a. we read the poem written in 1493 A.D.

b. We read the poem written in 1493 a.d.

c. We read the poem written in 1493 A.D.

4. a. When you return from your trip, I want a full report of your activities.

b. when you return from your trip, I want a full report of your activities.

c. When you return from your trip, i want a full report of your activities.

PROPER NOUNS AND PROPER ADJECTIVES

All proper nouns and proper adjectives—ones that name a specific person, place or thing—must be capitalized, but remembering which nouns and adjectives are proper can be difficult. The tables below lay out the most common categories of proper nouns and adjectives. Each section begins with a table that illustrates 5–7 related rules, followed by several practice exercises.

PROPER NOUNS, PART ONE	
Category of Proper Nouns	**Examples**
days of the week	Friday, Saturday
months	January, February
holidays	Christmas, Halloween
historical events, periods, documents	Civil War (historical event), Dark Ages (historical period), Declaration of Independence (document)
special events, calendar events	Pebble Beach Fall Classic, Renaissance Festival, Green River Days (special events); Labor Day, Father's Day (calendar events)
names of people and places	John Doe, Lincoln Center, Sears Tower

PRACTICE

Using the rules above, choose the correctly capitalized version of each of the following pairs.

5. a. Chaucer was one of the foremost poets from the Middle ages.

b. Chaucer was one of the foremost poets from the Middle Ages.

6. a. The Olsons spend Labor Day and four weeks of each summer at their lakeside cottage.

b. The Olsons spend Labor day and four weeks of each Summer at their Lakeside cottage.

7. a. We studied the declaration of independence in History class.

b. We studied the Declaration of Independence in history class.

8. a. Judy has two Uncles who fought in world war II.

b. Judy has two uncles who fought in World War II.

PROPER NOUNS, PART TWO	
Category of Proper Nouns	**Examples**
names of structures and buildings	Washington Memorial, Empire State Building
names of trains, ships, aircraft, and other modes of transportation	Queen Elizabeth, Discovery, Sioux Lines, TransWorld Airlines
names of products	Corn King hams, Dodge Intrepid
names of officials	Mayor Daley, President Clinton
works of art and literature	*Black Elk Speaks* (book), "Mending Wall" (poem), *Mona Lisa* (painting)
ethnic groups, races, languages, nationalities	Asian-American, Caucasian, French, Indian

PRACTICE

Choose the correctly capitalized version of each of the following pairs.

9. a. I enjoyed *spoon river anthology* by Edgar Lee Masters.

b. I enjoyed *Spoon River Anthology* by Edgar Lee Masters.

10. a. We caught a Vanguard Airlines flight to Orlando.

b. We caught a Vanguard airlines flight to Orlando.

11. a. The Talmud is a guide to the teachings of judaism.

b. The Talmud is a guide to the teachings of Judaism.

12. a. Paul has an editing job with Meredith publishing.

b. Paul has an Editing job with Meredith Publishing.

13. a. The university of iowa has an outstanding Law School.

b. The University of Iowa has an outstanding law school.

14. a. Dr. Gallagher researched her book at the Library of Congress.

b. Dr. Gallagher researched her book at the Library of congress.

PROPER NOUNS, PART THREE	
Category of Proper Nouns	**Examples**
cities, states, and governmental units	Des Moines, Iowa; Barrow, Alaska; Republic of South Africa
streets, highways, and roads	Grand Avenue, Interstate 29, Deadwood Road
landmarks and geographical locations	Continental Divide, Grand Canyon
public areas and bodies of water	Superior Forest, Missouri River
institutions, organizations, and businesses	Dartmouth College, Lions Club, Dodge Trucks

PRACTICE

Choose the correctly capitalized version of each of the following pairs.

15. a. In Switzerland, some citizens speak French, and others speak German.
  b. In switzerland, some citizens speak french, and others speak german.

16. a. Near a body of water called firth and forth, you can see Edinburgh, Scotland.
  b. Near a body of water called Firth and Forth, you can see Edinburgh, Scotland.

17. a. We drove along the Mississippi river to New Orleans.
  b. We drove along the Mississippi River to New Orleans.

18. a. Mount Everest, which is in the middle of the Himalayan Range, is the highest mountain in the world.
  b. Mount Everest, which is in the middle of the Himalayan Range, is the highest mountain in the World.

19. a. I have traveled on the Garden state Parkway, a main highway in New Jersey.
  b. I have traveled on the Garden State Parkway, a main highway in New Jersey.

PROPER ADJECTIVES

Proper adjectives are adjectives—that is, words that modify nouns—formed from a proper noun, often the name of a place. For instance, the proper noun *Canada* becomes the proper adjective *Canadian* when it modifies another noun, as in *Canadian bacon*. Note that the noun is not capitalized unless it is a proper noun in its own right.

Examples:

English muffin, Polish sausage, Japanese yen

PRACTICE

Choose the correctly capitalized version of each of the following pairs.

20. a. Some residents of ireland still speak the Gaelic Language.
  b. Some residents of Ireland still speak the Gaelic language.

21. a. Cortez, a Spanish explorer, conquered the Aztecs.
     b. Cortez, a spanish explorer, conquered the Aztecs.

22. a. The actress in the play tried to speak with a Scottish accent.
     b. The Actress in the play tried to speak with a Scottish accent.

23. a. I will never attempt to swim the English channel.
     b. I will never attempt to swim the English Channel.

24. a. I had never been to a Sri Lankan Restaurant before.
     b. I had never been to a Sri Lankan restaurant before.

WHEN NOT TO CAPITALIZE

Putting in capital letters where they don't belong is as bad as leaving them out where they do belong. Watch for these capitalization traps.

- Avoid unnecessarily capitalizing compass directions; however, direction words that refer to a specific area of the country should be capitalized.
  Examples:
    We headed **w**est after the Depression.
    The future of the country was cultivated in the **W**est.
- Avoid unnecessarily capitalizing the words referring to family members. Capitalize them only when they are used as names. If a possessive pronoun (*my, our, your, his, her, their*) comes before the word referring to a family member, the family word is not capitalized.
  Examples:
    When **U**ncle Harry visited last winter, none of my other **u**ncles came to see him.
    After my **m**other called me for lunch, **F**ather served the entree.
- Avoid unnecessarily capitalizing the seasons of the year or parts of the academic year.
  Example:
    If the university offers History of Education 405 in the **s**pring **s**emester, Horace will be able to graduate in May.
- Avoid unnecessarily capitalizing school subjects. They should be capitalized only if they are part of the name of a specific course.
  Examples:
    I try to avoid **m**ath courses because I'm not very good at them.
    Betsy is taking **A**lgebra II and **T**rigonometry I next semester.

- Avoid unnecessarily capitalizing words modified by proper adjectives.
  Examples:
  Polish **s**ausage, not Polish Sausage
  Mexican **r**estaurant, not Mexican Restaurant

PRACTICE

Choose the correctly capitalized version of each of the following pairs.

25. a. Digging the Canal through Panama took many years.
  b. Digging the canal through Panama took many years.

26. a. The Smoky Mountains are in the Southeastern part of the country.
  b. The Smoky Mountains are in the southeastern part of the country.

27. a. Nicholi Milani does more business in the East than in the West.
  b. Nicholi Milani does more business in the east than in the west.

28. a. The Midwest had the coldest winter on record in 1993.
  b. The midwest had the coldest winter on record in 1993.

29. a. Marianne had never been as far East as Columbus, Ohio.
  b. Marianne had never been as far east as Columbus, Ohio.

Skill Building Until Next Time

Find the obituaries in your local newspaper. Examine the capitalization used in the writing. How many of the rules you learned today can you find represented in a single obituary notice?

ANSWERS

1. c.	**9.** b.	**17.** b.	**25.** b.
2. b.	**10.** a.	**18.** a.	**26.** b.
3. c.	**11.** b.	**19.** b.	**27.** a.
4. a.	**12.** a.	**20.** b.	**28.** a.
5. b.	**13.** b.	**21.** a.	**29.** b.
6. a.	**14.** a.	**22.** a.	
7. b.	**15.** a.	**23.** b.	
8. b.	**16.** b.	**24.** b.	

L·E·S·S·O·N

PERIODS, QUESTION MARKS, AND EXCLAMATION POINTS

2

LESSON SUMMARY

This lesson shows you which punctuation marks to use to end sentences. These are sometimes referred to as "end marks." It also shows you other ways in which periods are used.

The exercise that follows reviews Lesson 1, Capitalization, and gives you an opportunity to see what you already know about periods and endmarks. Correct the capitalization in the **Problem** column on the next page, adding periods, question marks, and exclamation points where you think they should go. Check yourself with the **Solution** column as you go.

Problem

The supervisors at Meredith industrial thought Henry Simmons, jr. was a less than Ideal employee if he was at work on monday, He would most likely be absent on Tuesday, and he had an annoying habit of extending his Holidays, such as christmas and thanksgiving, a few extra days so he could rest from all the activities What a problem he was

during one particular holiday, he had traveled East to be with his family he called his supervisor on the Day he was to return to work and explained that the Flight Schedule at the Airport had been altered and that he would not be able to catch another flight that he could afford until the weekend (Three days away) what do you suppose happened His supervisor suggested that he rent a car and drive the 600 miles from williamsborough, pennsylvania, to centerville, ohio he said that the drive would be less expensive than a Plane Fare and that henry might be able to save his job if he were only one day late, rather than three

Henry decided to try the suggested plan he went to budget rental on Main street in williamsborough and rented a Ford tempo for the trip being a literary person, he also stopped at Banoff's bookstore to buy a Book on Tape by Garrison keillor called *the book of guys* listening to it was a Life-Altering Experience for henry because it taught him all the things his Father had forgotten to mention

Solution

The supervisors at Meredith Industrial thought Henry Simmons, Jr., was a less than ideal employee. If he was at work on Monday, he would most likely be absent on Tuesday, and he had an annoying habit of extending his holidays, such as Christmas and Thanksgiving, a few extra days so he could rest from all the activities. What a problem he was!

During one particular holiday, he had traveled east to be with his family. He called his supervisor on the day he was to return to work and explained that the flight schedule at the airport had been altered and that he would not be able to catch another flight that he could afford until the weekend (three days away). What do you suppose happened? His supervisor suggested that he rent a car and drive the 600 miles from Williamsborough, Pennsylvania, to Centerville, Ohio. He said that the drive would be less expensive than a plane fare and that Henry might be able to save his job if he were only one day late, rather than three.

Henry decided to try the suggested plan. He went to Budget Rental on Main Street in Williamsborough and rented a Ford Tempo for the trip. Being a literary person, he also stopped at Banoff's Bookstore to buy a book on tape by Garrison Keillor called *The Book of Guys*. Listening to it was a life-altering experience for Henry because it taught him all the things his father had forgotten to mention

(Continued on next page)

Problem (continued)

before henry became a man can you imagine that

In fact, henry was so inspired that he decided to pursue a Degree in philosophy at centerville community college he enrolled in history of Philosophy 203 during the Spring Semester by the end of may, henry was hooked on Education and has not missed a class nor a Day of Work since

Solution (continued)

before Henry became a man. Can you imagine that?

In fact, Henry was so inspired that he decided to pursue a degree in philosophy at Centerville Community College. He enrolled in History of Philosophy 203 during the spring semester. By the end of May, Henry was hooked on education and has not missed a class nor a day of work since.

RULES FOR USING PERIODS

- Use a period after an initial and after every part of an abbreviation, unless the abbreviation has become an acronym—an abbreviation that is pronounced as a word, such as AIDS—or a widely recognized name (TV, FBI, NATO, NASA). Titles—Mr., Ms., Dr., and so on—are also abbreviations that take periods. If the abbreviation comes at the end of a sentence, only one period is needed.
  Examples:
  The tour leaves on **Mon., Jan.** 1, at 3 P.M.
  The book was written by **C. S.** Lewis.
  A. J. Mandelli researched brain function for the **FBI.**
- Use a period before a decimal and between dollars and cents.
  Examples:
  A gallon equals **3.875** liters.
  The new textbook costs **$54.75.**
  Only **5.6** percent of our consumers spend over **$100.00** per month on our products.
- Use a period at the end of a sentence that makes a statement.
  Examples:
  Henry Kissinger served under two U. S. presidents.
  Wilson will lecture in the forum after school today.
  Many consider P. T. Barnum the best salesman ever to have walked the earth.
- Use a period at the end of a sentence that makes a request, gives an instruction, or states a command.
  Examples:
  Empty the kitchen trash before you take the garbage out.
  Turn right at the first stop light, and then go to the second house on the left.

- Use a period at the end of a sentence that asks an indirect question.

  Examples:

  My neighbor asked if we had seen his cat. (The direct question was, "Have you seen my cat?")

  Quentin wanted to know how we had arrived at that answer. (The direct question was, "How did you arrive at that answer?")

PRACTICE

Choose the correctly written version from each of the following sets of sentences. You will find the answers to each set of questions at the end of the lesson.

1. a. The train passed through Rockford, Ill., on its way to St. Joseph, Mo.
   b. The train passed through Rockford, Ill, on its way to St Joseph, Mo.
   c. The train passed through Rockford, Ill, on its way to St. Joseph, Mo.

2. a. Ms Cory Ames, Dr Matthew Olson, and H. J. Lane went to Chicago, Ill..
   b. Ms Cory Ames, Dr Matthew Olson, and HJ Lane went to Chicago, Ill.
   c. Ms. Cory Ames, Dr. Matthew Olson, and H. J. Lane went to Chicago, Ill.

3. a. The bedrooms measured 12 ft. by 14 ft.
   b. The bedrooms measured 12 ft by 14 ft.
   c. The bedrooms measured 12 ft. by 14 ft..

4. a. Bob asked if the price of the CD was $13.98?
   b. Bob asked if the price of the CD was $13.98.
   c. Bob asked if the price of the CD was $1398¢.

5. a. Tie your shoe. Before you trip and break a leg.
   b. Tie your shoe before you trip and break a leg.
   c. Tie your shoe before you trip and break a leg

6. a. Mr and Mrs Fletcher visited 10 cities in 20 days.
   b. Mr. and Mrs. Fletcher visited 10 cities in 20 days.
   c. Mr and Mrs. Fletcher visited 10 cities in 20 days.

7. a. Mayor and Mrs. Dorian will address the city council at 8:00 PM
   b. Mayor and Mrs Dorian will address the city council at 8:00 P.M.
   c. Mayor and Mrs. Dorian will address the city council at 8:00 P.M.

8. a. Oh, all right. Tell me your riddle.

b. Oh. all right. Tell me your riddle.

c. Oh, all right Tell me your riddle.

RULES FOR USING QUESTION MARKS AND EXCLAMATION POINTS

■ Use a question mark after a word or group of words that asks a question even if it is not a complete sentence.

Examples:

What did you do last night?

Will you put out the trash?

Okay?

May we go to the movies after we've finished our homework?

Are we?

■ Use an exclamation point after a sentence that expresses strong feeling.

Examples:

Look out for that car!

I just can't stand the smell in here!

A word of caution about exclamation points to show strong feeling: Exclamation points are a little bit like salt on food. Most people like a little bit. Nobody likes too much.

■ Use an exclamation point after an interjection—a word or phrase expressing strong feeling—when it is written as a single sentence.

Examples:

Doggone it!

Yikes!

■ Use an exclamation point after a sentence that begins with a question word but doesn't ask a question.

Examples:

What a dunce I am!

How marvelous of you to come!

PRACTICE

Choose the correctly written version of each of the following sets of sentences.

9. a. Help! I'm falling?

b. Help! I'm falling.

c. Help! I'm falling!

10. a. I can't believe how naive I was!
b. I can't believe how naive I was.
c. I can't believe how naive I was?

11. a. The auditor asked me why I didn't save the receipts?
b. The auditor asked me why I didn't save the receipts.
c. The auditor asked me why I didn't save the receipts!

12. a. Can you tell me the seating capacity of this meeting room.
b. Can you tell me the seating capacity of this meeting room?
c. Can you tell me the seating capacity of this meeting room!

13. a. How utterly disgusting this movie is.
b. How utterly disgusting this movie is?
c. How utterly disgusting this movie is!

14. a. Was Alexander the Great born in 350 B.C.
b. Was Alexander the great born in 350 B.C.?
c. Was Alexander the Great born in 350 B.C.?

15. a. Our group will meet at the library at 10:00 P.M. to research T. S. Eliot.
b. Our group will meet at the library at 10:00 PM to research T. S. Eliot.
c. Our group will meet at the library at 10:00 P.M. to research TS. Eliot.

16. a. Is this sweater $59.95 or $69.95?
b. Is this sweater $59.95 or $69.95.
c. Is this sweater $5995 or $6995?

17. a. Wow. What a close call that was?
b. Wow! What a close call that was.
c. Wow! What a close call that was!

18. a. Those carpenters. Do you know how much they charged?
b. Those carpenters? Do you know how much they charged?
c. Those carpenters! Do you know how much they charged?

Skill Building Until Next Time

Take a few minutes to practice what you have learned today. If you are reading a book right now, look through a few of the pages until you find at least three examples of each type of endmark you learned about today. Are the endmarks used according to the rules you used today? If you're not currently reading a book, just grab one from the shelf at home or at school.

ANSWERS

1. a.	**6.** b.	**11.** b.	**16.** a.
2. c.	**7.** c.	**12.** b.	**17.** c.
3. a.	**8.** a.	**13.** c.	**18.** c.
4. b.	**9.** c.	**14.** c.	
5. b.	**10.** a.	**15.** a.	

AVOIDING FAULTY SENTENCES

3

LESSON SUMMARY

This lesson will help you distinguish between complete sentences and faulty sentences so that you can avoid writing sentence fragments, run-on sentences and comma splices.

Begin your study of complete sentences by looking at the **Problem** paragraph that appears on the next page. Underline the groups of words that form complete sentences. See if you can distinguish them from the fragments, run-ons, and comma splices included in the paragraph. Then check your work against the **Solution** paragraph, also on the next page, where the complete sentences are underlined.

Problem

Just the other day I came home from work as excited as I had ever been. The night before someone from Publisher's Clearinghouse had called. To tell me that I would be receiving a prize package worth potentially millions of dollars. I was so excited because, unlike other offers, this really sounded legitimate, it sounded to me as though I might really win something this time. I hastily opened the mailbox. Hoping to find the promised envelope. There it was. Between the *Life* magazine and the Fingerhut catalog. The promised letter. When I finally finished reading the entire mailing. I realized my chances were really no better with this contest than they had been for any other contest I had entered in the past and I was disappointed that I had spent so much time reading all of the material then I threw it all in the recycling basket and went to bed. Dejected.

Solution

Just the other day I came home from work as excited as I had ever been. The night before someone from Publisher's Clearinghouse had called. To tell me that I would be receiving a prize package worth potentially millions of dollars. I was so excited because, unlike other offers, this really sounded legitimate, it sounded to me as though I might really win something this time. I hastily opened the mailbox. Hoping to find the promised envelope. There it was. Between the *Life* magazine and the Fingerhut catalog. The promised letter. When I finally finished reading the entire mailing. I realized my chances were really no better with this contest than they had been for any other contest I had entered in the past and I was disappointed that I had spent so much time reading all of the material then I threw it all in the recycling basket and went to bed. Dejected.

COMPLETE SENTENCES

A complete sentence is a group of words that meets all three of the following criteria:

1. It has a verb (a word or phrase that explains an action such as *want, run, take, give,* or a state of being, such as *am, is, are, was, were, be*). Many sentences have more than one verb. The verbs in the sentences below are highlighted for you.

Examples:
Bob and Alexandra both **want** a promotion. (action verb)
Yurika **drafted** a memo and **sent** it to the sales department. (action verbs)
Herbert and Tan **are** the chief operators in this department. (state of being verb)

2. It has a subject (someone or something that performs the action or serves as the main focus of the sentence). As with verbs, many sentences have more than one subject.

Examples:

Bob and **Alexandra** both want a promotion.

Yurika drafted a memo and sent it to the sales department.

Herbert and **Tan** are the chief operators in this department.

3. It expresses a complete thought. In other words, the group of words has a completed meaning. Sometimes a group of words has both a subject and a verb but still does not express a complete thought. Look at the following examples. The subjects and verbs are highlighted to make them easier to identify.

Complete sentences (also called independent clauses):

I left an hour earlier than usual.

Our **team finished** its year-end evaluation.

Roger tried to explain his position.

Sentence fragments (dependent clauses):

If **I left** an hour earlier than usual.

When our **team finished** its year-end evaluation.

Whenever **Roger tried** to explain his position.

The next section explains why the groups of words in the second set are not complete sentences.

SENTENCE FRAGMENTS

In the last set of examples above, you may have noticed that each fragment is longer than the similar complete sentence. The groups of words are otherwise the same, but the fragments have an extra word at the beginning. These words are called *subordinating conjunctions*. If a group of words that would normally be a complete sentence is preceded by a subordinating conjunction, something more is needed to complete the thought. These *subordinate* or *dependent clauses* need something more to complete their meaning; therefore, they *depend* on an *independent clause*, a group of words that by itself could form a complete sentence. Examine how the fragments from above have been rewritten below to express a complete thought.

If I left an hour earlier than usual, I would be able to avoid rush hour.

When our team finished its year-end evaluation, we all took the next day off.

Whenever Roger tried to explain his position, he misquoted the facts.

These words can be used as subordinating conjunctions:

after	once	until
although	since	when
as	than	whenever
because	that	where
before	though	wherever
if	unless	while

Sometimes a subordinating conjunction is a phrase rather than a single word:

as if we didn't already know
as though she had always lived in the town
as long as they can still be heard
as soon as I can finish my work
even though you aren't quite ready
in order that we may proceed more carefully
so that all of us understand exactly

Subordinate clauses used as sentences are only one type of sentence fragment. Look at the questions below. For each question, choose the group of words that forms a complete sentence and put the corresponding letter in the box at the right. See if you notice any similarities among the groups of words that are fragments.

	Word Group A	**Word Group B**	**?**
1.	We are ready for the next task.	Washing the car.	☐
2.	Seeing the plane arriving.	Heather's family rushed to the gate.	☐
3.	Broken down after years of use.	The receptionist finally got a new phone.	☐
4.	We saw Andrea sitting all by herself.	Imagining what Florida was like in March.	☐

The complete sentences are 1. A, 2. B, 3. B, and 4. A. The fragments are simply phrases. They do not contain a subject or a verb. If you combine the two sets of words, both will be part of a complete sentence. See how this is done in the examples below. With some of the sentences, all that is needed is a comma. With others, a few extra words must be added to incorporate the phrase into the rest of the sentence.

1. We are ready for the next task, which is washing the car.

2. Seeing the plane arriving, Heather's family rushed to the gate.

3. Since the phone was broken down after years of use, the receptionist finally got a new one.

4. We saw Andrea sitting all by herself, imagining what Florida was like in March.

Now look at the table below. In each set, one of the options is a complete sentence. The other is a fragment. Put the letter of the complete sentences in the box at the far right. See if you notice any similarities among the fragments.

Word Group A	Word Group B	?
1. About the way he combs his hair.	I've noticed something very strange.	☐
2. My aunt is a respiratory therapist.	A person who helps people rebuild their lungs and circulatory system.	☐
3. Benjamin saw a piece of key lime pie.	His favorite type of dessert.	☐
4. And tried to sell popcorn and candy.	We went door to door.	☐
5. During the rest of the afternoon.	Everything went smoothly.	☐
6. Icy roads and hazardous weather.	We couldn't make the deadline.	☐
7. In the parking ramp near our building.	I was fortunate to find a parking spot.	☐
8. And saw the picture of our company's new owner.	We read the morning paper.	☐
9. We traveled through the desert all night.	Without seeing a single car or building.	☐
10. We walked all over downtown.	And applied for part-time jobs at theaters.	☐

The complete sentences are 1. B, 2. A, 3. A, 4. B, 5. B, 6. B, 7. B, 8. B, 9. A, and 10. A.

Most of the fragments are phrases that can easily be incorporated into a complete sentence using the independent clause with which they are paired. Try to do this yourself. Compare your sentences with the versions below.

Look at sentences 1, 5, 7, and 9. The fragments in these sentences were nothing more than phrases separated from the independent clauses. All you need to do is add the fragment to the complete sentence in a spot where it fits. No punctuation or additional words are needed.

1. I've noticed something very strange about the way he combs his hair.

5. Everything went smoothly during the rest of the afternoon.

7. I was fortunate to find a spot in the parking ramp near our building.

9. We traveled through the desert all night without seeing a single car or building.

Now examine sentences 2 and 3. These fragments are phrases that explain or further identify something in the complete sentence. Such phrases are called *appositive* phrases. All you need to do is place a comma after the word being explained or identified, and then add the appositive phrase.

2. My aunt is a respiratory therapist, a person who helps people rebuild their lungs and respiratory system.

3. Benjamin saw key lime pie, his favorite type of dessert.

Take a look at sentences 4, 8, and 10. In these sentences, the fragment is a verb (action) separated from the independent clause or the complete sentence. All that is required is to add the fragment to the sentence.

4. We went door to door and tried to sell popcorn and candy.

8. We read the morning paper and saw the picture of our company's new owner.

10. We walked all over downtown and applied for part-time jobs at theaters.

Finally, look at the remaining sentence, 6. In this sentence, extra words are needed to add the fragment to the sentence.

6. We couldn't make the deadline because of the icy roads and hazardous weather.

RUN-ON SENTENCES

An *independent clause* is a group of words that could be a complete sentence all by itself. A *run-on sentence* is one in which independent clauses have been run together without punctuation (a period, semicolon, or comma).

Examples:

Lynn moved from Minneapolis her job was transferred.

The concert seemed unending it lasted almost until midnight.

We got some gas then we headed off to Omaha.

All three of these examples can be corrected quite easily in one of three ways:

- By adding a period and a capital letter.

  Lynn moved from Minneapolis. Her job was transferred.

  The concert seemed unending. It lasted almost until midnight.

  We got some gas. Then we headed off to Omaha.

- By adding a comma and a conjunction (*and, but, or, for, nor, yet, so*). Sometimes you have to change the order of the words.

  Lynn's job was transferred, and she moved from Minneapolis.

  The concert seemed unending, for it lasted almost until midnight.

  We got some gas, and then we headed off to Omaha.

■ By turning one of the independent clauses into a dependent clause. To do this you need to add a subordinating conjunction where it fits in the sentence. This can usually be done in several different ways by rewording the clauses or by using different subordinating conjunctions. Remember the list of subordinating conjunction you saw earlier in this lesson?

Lynn moved from Minneapolis because her job was transferred.

When her job was transferred, Lynn moved from Minneapolis.

Since the concert lasted almost until midnight, it seemed unending.

The concert seemed unending because it lasted until almost midnight.

After we got some gas, we headed off to Omaha.

We headed off to Omaha after we got some gas.

PRACTICE

Choose the answers that include *only* complete sentences. Watch for fragments as well as run-ons. Answers are at the end of the lesson.

1. a. The huge northern pike snapped my line. And took my favorite lure.
   b. The huge northern pike snapped my line and took my favorite lure.

2. a. Cathy is a good organizer. She chairs the newly formed committee.
   b. Cathy is a good organizer she chairs the newly formed committee.

3. a. The lights were on in the house we assumed you were at home.
   b. The lights were on in the house. We assumed you were at home.

4. a. Andy showed a great deal of promise. After only his first month of work.
   b. Andy showed a great deal of promise after only his first month of work.

5. a. You will find the manual inside the right-hand drawer of my desk.
   b. You will find the manual. Inside the right-hand drawer of my desk.

6. a. Sally needs additional time to complete the project it is more complicated than we thought.
   b. Sally needs additional time to complete the project. It is more complicated than we thought.

7. a. After Mavis wrote the program, Sam edited it.
   b. Mavis wrote the program Sam edited it.

8. a. Bob signed the application he gave it to the interviewer.
   b. Bob signed the application, and he gave it to the interviewer.

9. a. Edsel was ready for the auditor his department's books were all in order.

b. Edsel was ready for the auditor since his department's books were all in order.

10. a. Alexis found a part-time job that supplemented her income.

b. Alexis found a part-time job. Supplemented her income.

COMMA SPLICES

A *comma splice* is the last kind of sentence fault you will study today. It is actually a special type of run-on sentence in which a comma is used in place of a semicolon to join two independent clauses without a conjunction. A comma splice can be corrected by putting a semicolon in place of the comma or by adding a conjunction after the comma.

Wrong

Henry lives across the street, he has been there for 25 years.

Correct

Henry lives across the street; he has been there for 25 years.

Henry lives across the street, and he has been there for 25 years.

Wrong

Mary heads the search committee, John is the recorder.

Correct

Mary heads the search committee; John is the recorder.

Mary heads the search committee, and John is the recorder.

Wrong

Sid gave demonstrations all summer long, he returned in the fall.

Correct

Sid gave demonstrations all summer long; he returned in the fall.

Sid gave demonstrations all summer long, but he returned in the fall.

PRACTICE

Here is an opportunity to apply what you have learned about complete sentences, fragments, run-ons, and comma splices. In each of the numbered items below, decide whether the group of words is a correctly written sentence or sentences (S), a fragment (F), a run-on sentence (ROS), or a comma splice (CS). Write the label next to each number, and then check your work against the answer key at the end of the lesson. You may recognize some of these sentences from the opening example paragraph. By now, you know how to correct the ones that were not complete sentences.

11. Dr. Anders left detailed care instructions for the patient. A personal friend of his.

12. The night before someone from Publisher's Clearinghouse had called. To tell me that I would be receiving a prize package worth potentially millions of dollars.

13. I was so excited because unlike the other offers, this really sounded legitimate, it sounded to me as though I might really win something this time.

14. I hastily opened the mailbox. Hoping to find the promised envelope.

15. There it was. The promised letter.

16. When I finally finished reading the entire mailing.

17. The officer responded to the call, he received it at 8:10 P.M.

18. Emily posted the last transaction it was time to close the books for the day.

19. Our new computer system is still not working properly.

20. Hanging over the doorway in the office next to the conference room.

Rewrite the fragments, run-ons, and comma splices as complete sentences in the space below.

Skill Building Until Next Time

Go back to the paragraph at the beginning of the lesson. Revise it to eliminate the sentence fragments, comma splices, and run-on sentences. As you read the morning paper or written material at work or school, look for sentence faults. If you find none, look for complete sentences that could be combined. Chances are you'll find plenty of those in a newspaper. You can also find plenty of sentence faults, especially fragments, in advertisements. Practice writing complete sentences in any written work you are assigned.

ANSWERS

1. b.	**6.** b.	**11.** F	**16.** F
2. a.	**7.** a.	**12.** F	**17.** CS
3. b.	**8.** b.	**13.** CS	**18.** ROS
4. b.	**9.** b.	**14.** F	**19.** S
5. a.	**10.** a.	**15.** F	**20.** F

L·E·S·S·O·N 4

COMMAS AND SENTENCE PARTS

LESSON SUMMARY

This lesson and the next one deal with commas. Today's lesson is about how commas relate to the parts of sentences, such as clauses and phrases.

D uring this lesson you will learn how to use commas in relationship to sentence parts. As you progress through this lesson, remember what you have learned about sentences and sentence faults in Lesson 3. Before you begin this lesson, see how much you already know about commas and sentence parts. Insert commas where you think they should be in the **Problem** version of the sentences that appear on the next page. Check yourself against the corrected version of the sentences in the **Solution** section that follows.

Problem	Solution
Startled I looked up to see a bird flying around the office.	Startled, I looked up to see a bird flying around the office.
After examining the report carefully Edith printed a final copy and mailed it.	After examining the report carefully, Edith printed a final copy and mailed it.
As soon as we finish this last round we can quit for the day.	As soon as we finish this last round, we can quit for the day.
Thinking carefully about the needs of the customers Randall revised his sales plan.	Thinking carefully about the needs of the customers, Randall revised his sales plan.
Because production falls during the winter months we will cut one daily shift.	Because production falls during the winter months, we will cut one daily shift.
Like a confused duckling Richard waddled through the mound of paperwork.	Like a confused duckling, Richard waddled through the mound of paperwork.
She spends a great deal of time listening to the problems of her customers who have come to depend on her advice.	She spends a great deal of time listening to the problems of her customers, who have come to depend on her advice.
Zig Ziglar the last motivational speaker brought the convention crowd to their feet.	Zig Ziglar, the last motivational speaker, brought the convention crowd to their feet.
The cable car which I am waiting for is already twenty minutes late.	The cable car, which I am waiting for, is already twenty minutes late.

COMMAS FOLLOWING INTRODUCTORY WORDS, PHRASES, AND CLAUSES

Use a comma to set off introductory words, phrases, and clauses from the main part of a sentence. The comma keeps a reader from accidentally attaching the introductory portion to the main part of the sentence and having to go back and reread the sentence. In other words, commas following introductory elements will save the reader time and reduce the chances of misinterpreting what you write. Examine the examples below to see how introductory words, phrases, and clauses are set off with commas.

Words:

Disappointed, we left the movie before it ended.

Annoyed, the manager stomped back into the storeroom.

Amazed, Captain Holland dismissed the rest of the troops.

Phrases:

Expecting the worst, we liquidated most of our inventory.

Badly injured in the accident, the president was gone for two months.

Reluctant to make matters any worse, the doctor called in a specialist.

Clauses:

If we plan carefully for the grand opening, we can increase sales.

While we were eating lunch, an important fax came.

Because we left before the meeting ended, we were not eligible to win a door prize.

Remember the fragment section of Lesson 3? One part of it dealt with subordinate or dependent clauses. Subordinate or dependent clauses are what you see in the last set of examples above. The first part of each sentence, the subordinate or dependent clause, is followed by a comma. The two parts of each of these sentences could very easily be reversed and the sentence would still make sense. However, if you reverse the sentence parts, making the independent clause the first clause in the sentence, you would NOT need a comma.

Subordinate clauses *after* the independent clause:

We can increase sales if we plan carefully for the grand opening.

An important fax came while we were eating lunch.

We were not eligible to win a door prize because we left before the meeting ended.

PRACTICE

Choose the correctly written sentence from each of the following pairs. Answers are provided at the end of the lesson.

1. a. Content for the first time in his life, Bryce returned to school.
   b. Content for the first time in his life Bryce returned to school.

2. a. As far as I'm concerned we can call this project a success.
   b. As far as I'm concerned, we can call this project a success.

3. a. I will never forget this moment, as long as I live.
   b. I will never forget this moment as long as I live.

4. a. By the time we finally made up our minds, the contract had been awarded to someone else.
   b. By the time we finally made up our minds the contract had been awarded to someone else.

5. a. Indignant, Mr. Caster left the restaurant without leaving a tip.
   b. Indignant Mr. Caster left the restaurant without leaving a tip.

6. a. Wayne was delighted when he found out he'd been awarded the leading role in the show.

b. Wayne was delighted, when he found out he'd been awarded the leading role in the show.

7. a. By designing the program ourselves, we saved a great deal of expense.

b. By designing the program ourselves we saved a great deal of expense.

8. a. I began working for this company, before I was sixteen.

b. Before I was sixteen, I began working for this company.

9. a. Dripping with water from head to toe, Angie climbed the bank of the river.

b. Dripping with water from head to toe Angie climbed the bank of the river.

10. a. The company honored its oldest employee at the annual meeting.

b. The company honored its oldest employee, at the annual meeting.

Commas help a reader to know which words belong together. Add commas to the following sentences to help make their meaning clear.

1. Inside the house was clean and tastefully decorated.

2. After running the greyhounds settled back into their boxes.

3. Alone at night time seems endless.

4. As he watched the game slowly came to an end.

You should have marked the sentences like this:

1. Inside, the house was clean and tastefully decorated.

2. After running, the greyhounds settled back into their boxes.

3. Alone at night, time seems endless.

4. As he watched, the game slowly came to an end.

COMMAS WITH APPOSITIVES

An *appositive* is a word or group of words that immediately follows a noun or pronoun. The appositive makes the noun or pronoun clearer or more definite by explaining or identifying it. Look at these examples. The appositives and appositive phrases have been highlighted.

Examples:

Rachel Stein won the first prize, **an expense-paid vacation to the Bahamas.**

New Orleans, **home of the Saints,** is one of my favorite cities.

One of the most inspiring motivators in college basketball is Dr. Tom Davis, **coach of the Iowa Hawkeyes.**

Sometimes a proper name that identifies or further explains will follow a noun or pronoun. Although this is also a type of appositive, it is not set off by commas.

Examples:

My sister **Deb** lives four hours away.

The noted novelist **Barbara Kingsolver** writes about the South and Southwest.

The president **Manuel Diaz** will visit this site tomorrow.

Place commas where they are needed in the following sentences.

1. *Megabyte,* a word virtually unheard of a decade ago is very common today.

2. Mrs. McCord the investment specialist left a message for you this afternoon.

3. Jane likes to spend Saturday mornings at the local farmer's market a feast for the senses.

4. Water purity a major concern for campers has steadily worsened over the years.

5. High heels were invented by Louis XIV a very short French king.

6. My aunt Marsha will visit later this month.

You should have marked the sentences like this:

1. *Megabyte,* a word virtually unheard of a decade ago, is very common today.

2. Mrs. McCord, the investment specialist, left a message for you this afternoon.

3. Jane likes to spend Saturday mornings at the local farmer's market, a feast for the senses.

4. Water purity, a major concern for campers, has steadily worsened over the years.

5. High heels were invented by Louis XIV, a very short French king.

6. My aunt Marsha will visit later this month. (no comma needed)

COMMAS AND NONRESTRICTIVE CLAUSES

Earlier in this lesson you learned that a subordinate clause at the beginning of a sentence is followed by a comma, but a subordinate clause any other place in the sentence is not set off by a comma. This is true only if the clause is an essential clause. In some sentences a clause cannot be omitted without changing the basic meaning of the sentences. Omitting such a clause changes the meaning of the sentence or makes it untrue. Such a clause is called an *essential* or *restrictive* clause.

Example:

All drivers **who have had a drunk driving conviction** should have their licenses revoked.

All drivers should have their licenses revoked.

The highlighted clause is essential because the meaning of the sentence is changed drastically if the clause is removed from the sentence. A restrictive clause is not set off with commas.

However, a *nonessential* or *nonrestrictive* clause needs to be set off by commas. A clause is nonrestrictive if it simply adds information that is not essential to the basic meaning of the sentence. If a nonrestrictive clause is removed, the basic meaning of the sentence is not changed.

Example:

My father, **who is still farming,** is 74 years old.

My father is 74 years old.

The highlighted clause is nonrestrictive. If it is removed from the sentence, the basic meaning of the sentence is not changed. Nonrestrictive clauses usually begin with one of these subordinating conjunctions: *who, whom, whose, which,* or *that.* (Technically, the proper subordinating conjunction for a restrictive clause is *that,* while nonrestrictive clauses use *which,* but in practice many writers ignore this distinction.)

PRACTICE

Each of the sentences in the table below contains a subordinate clause. These are highlighted for you. If the clause is restrictive, or essential, write R in the box at the right. If the clause is nonrestrictive, or nonessential, put N in the box and set the clause off with commas. Answers are at the end of the lesson.

11. Matt **who loves to play video games** is interested in a computer science career. ☐

12. My grandfather **who was born in Berlin** speaks with a German accent. ☐

13. James **who is very shy** had a great deal of trouble with his first speech. ☐

14. The hotel pays the parking ramp fees for anyone **who is a registered guest.** ☐

15. People **who are born on February 29** grow old more slowly than the rest of us. ☐

16. Animals **that have backbones** are called vertebrates. ☐

17. Nicotine **which is present in tobacco products** is a powerful poison.

18. Many Scandinavian names end with sen or son **both of which mean son of.**

19. We live on Fleur Drive **which is right next to the airport.**

20. Mrs. Olson is not a teacher **who takes homework lightly.**

REVIEW

This next exercise reviews everything you have learned so far. The passage below contains no commas, endmarks, or capitalization. Use what you have learned so far to add capitalization, endmarks, and commas to make sense of the **Problem** version of the passage. Check your work against the **Solution** version that follows.

Problem

even though peter liked his job a great deal he always looked forward to his summer vacation it was the highlight of his year usually he spent two weeks in the middle of july at camp wi wi ta which was forty miles from his home he was responsible for six physically challenged children for 24 hrs a day for two wks how he loved camp

peter took the counseling job one he loved dearly very seriously each morning he rose before the first child awoke and never went to bed until the last of his kids went to sleep at night the best part of the job was challenging the kids to do things for themselves peter would insist that they comb their hair or cut their own food even if they begged for help the camp dean and some of the other counselors thought peter was slacking on the job but he didn't see it that way he enjoyed knowing that his kids left camp more capable and confident than they had been when they arrived

Solution

Even though Peter liked his job a great deal, he always looked forward to his summer vacation. It was the highlight of his year. Usually, he spent two weeks in the middle of July at Camp Wi Wi Ta, which was forty miles from his home. He was responsible for six physically challenged children for 24 hrs. a day for two wks. How he loved camp!

Peter took the counseling job, one he loved dearly, very seriously. Each morning he rose before the first child awoke and never went to bed until the last of his kids went to sleep at night. The best part of the job was challenging the kids to do things for themselves. Peter would insist that they comb their hair or cut their own food even if they begged for help. The camp dean and some of the other counselors thought Peter was slacking on the job, but he didn't see it that way. He enjoyed knowing that his kids left camp more capable and confident than they had been when they arrived.

Skill Building Until Next Time

As you've seen in this lesson, omitting commas before introductory elements or wrongly placing commas around restrictive clauses can lead to humorous misreadings. Write some sentences of your own that are hard to read without commas, like this: "As they ate the horse moved closer." Then correct them by adding commas.

ANSWERS

1. a.
2. b.
3. b.
4. a.
5. a.
6. a.
7. a.
8. b.
9. a.
10. a.
11. N Matt, who loves to play video games, is interested in a computer science career.
12. N My grandfather, who was born in Berlin, speaks with a German accent.

13. N James, who is very shy, had a great deal of trouble with his first speech.
14. R No commas are needed.
15. R No commas are needed.
16. R No commas are needed.
17. N Nicotine, which is present in tobacco products, is a powerful poison.
18. N Many Scandinavian names end with *son* or *sen*, both of which mean *son of*.
19. N We live on Fleur Drive, which is right next to the airport.
20. R No commas are needed.

L·E·S·S·O·N

COMMAS THAT SEPARATE

5

LESSON SUMMARY

Besides setting off sentence parts, commas are used in many other situations. This lesson reviews the many instances in which you should use commas to separate sentence elements.

Commas are used to separate or clarify relationships between sentence parts in order to make the meaning of a sentence clear and easy to grasp. In this lesson you'll learn how to use commas to separate independent clauses, items in a series, items in a date or address, two or more adjectives preceding a noun, and contrasting elements and words that interrupt the flow of thought in a sentence. The last section of the lesson explains how to use commas in the greetings and closings of a friendly letter.

Begin by seeing how much you already know about commas that separate. Add commas where you think they are needed to the **Problem** column on the next page. Check yourself against the corrected version in the **Solution** column. Try to identify the rules that apply to those you missed as you go through the lesson.

Problem

Dear Aunt Jan

    I hate to give you my whole life story so I'll start halfway through. When I began my first full-time job I was twenty-one years old a freshly scrubbed college graduate. I worked as an English teacher at Sioux Valley Schools 721 Straight Row Drive Linn Grove Iowa. My first day of teacher workshops was August 28 1976 and I came armed with a nice clean notebook a pen a pencil and a new three-ring binder. I expected a day of meetings but I got nothing of the sort. The only time the entire staff got together was at noon when the principal announced that the parents group had set up a lunch for us in the cafeteria. What a feast: fresh sweet corn vine-ripened tomatoes new potatoes and grilled hamburgers. The president of the school board cooked the burgers nothing less than prime Iowa beef to perfection. It was a first day as you might imagine that I will never forget. I'm looking forward to your next letter.

Sincerely

Solution

Dear Aunt Jan,

    I hate to give you my whole life story, so I'll start halfway through. When I began my first full-time job, I was twenty-one years old, a freshly scrubbed college graduate. I worked as an English teacher at Sioux Valley Schools, 721 Straight Row Drive, Linn Grove, Iowa. My first day of teacher workshops was August 28, 1976, and I came armed with a nice, clean notebook, a pen, a pencil and a new three-ring binder. I expected a day of meetings, but I got nothing of the sort. The only time the entire staff got together was at noon when the principal announced that the parents' group had set up a lunch for us in the cafeteria. What a feast: fresh sweet corn, vine-ripened tomatoes, new potatoes and grilled hamburgers. The president of the school board cooked the burgers, nothing less than prime Iowa beef, to perfection. It was a first day, as you might imagine, that I will never forget. I'm looking forward to your next letter.

Sincerely,

COMMAS WITH INDEPENDENT CLAUSES JOINED BY A CONJUNCTION

As you may recall from Lesson 3, an *independent clause* is a group of words that could stand alone as a complete sentence. A *conjunction* is a joining word: *and, but, or, for, nor, so,* or *yet.* Sometimes a writer will combine two or more independent clauses to form a compound sentence. If a conjunction joins the clauses, place a comma after the first clause. The commas and conjunctions are highlighted in the following examples.

Examples:

I went to bed early last night, **so** I felt rested this morning.

The city's economic situation has improved, **but** there are still neighborhoods where many people depend on the generosity of others in order to live.

Susan worked through lunch, **and** now she is able to leave the office early.

If independent clauses are joined *without* a conjunction, they are separated by a semicolon instead of a comma.

Examples:

I went to bed early last night; I felt rested this morning.

The city's economic situation has improved; however, there are still neighborhoods where many people depend on the generosity of others in order to live.

Susan worked through lunch; now she is able to leave the office early.

PRACTICE

Use commas and semicolons to correctly punctuate the following sentences. Answers are at the end of the lesson.

1. You can safely view an eclipse through the viewing glass of a welding helmet or you can look through a piece of overexposed film.

2. The prisoner showed no remorse as the guilty verdict was announced nor did the tears of the victim's family arouse any emotion.

3. The young calf put its head over the fence and it licked my hand and sucked on my fingers.

4. Icebergs in the Antarctic are flat and smooth but those in the Arctic are rough.

5. I understand your position on this issue I still believe you are dead wrong.

6. I like Sam he likes me for we are best of friends.

7. The inventory is valued at one million dollars but it's not enough to cover our debt.

8. If you know of anyone with data processing experience encourage him or her to apply for this new position.

COMMAS TO SEPARATE ITEMS IN A SERIES

Commas are used to separate items in lists of similar words, phrases, or clauses in order to make the material easier for a reader to understand. The last item in a series is also usually preceded by a conjunction. Strictly speaking, no comma is needed before the conjunction. (However, many writers—some test writers included—prefer to use a comma before the final conjunction to avoid confusion.)

Examples:

Al, Jane, Herbert, and Willis all applied for the promotion.

The old Tempo's engine squealed loudly, shook violently, and ground to a halt.

The instructions clearly showed how to assemble the equipment, how to load the software, and how to boot the system.

If each item in the series is separated by a conjunction, no commas are needed.

Example:

Billie and Charles and Cameron performed at the company Christmas party.

COMMAS TO SEPARATE ITEMS IN A DATE OR AN ADDRESS

When giving a complete date in the format *month-day-year*, put a comma on either side of the year. When giving a date that is only a month and year, no comma is needed.

Use a comma to separate each element of an address, such as the street address, city, state, and country. A comma is also used after the state or country if the sentence continues after the address.

Examples:

We moved from Fayetteville, North Carolina, on May 16, 1993.

Since November 1994, Terry has lived at 654 36th Street, Lincoln, Nebraska.

Dwana attended Drake University, Des Moines, Iowa, both fall 1994 and spring 1995.

PRACTICE

Add commas and endmarks where they are needed to the following sentences. Use not only what you are learning in this lesson but also what you learned in Lesson 4. Answers appear at the end of the lesson.

9. After he ran into the mayor's car with his truck Adam used his cellular phone to call the police his doctor his lawyer and his insurance agent.

10. The homegrown philosopher who lives next door at 251 Acorn Street Libertyville Kansas claims to know exactly who invented the wheel sliced bread and kissing.

11. Estelle was born on January 31 1953 and Arun was born on June 30 1960.

12. Looking for a solution to the printing problem Karissa asked an older employee questioned the supervisor and finally consulted the printer manual.

13. Baruch brought a jello salad to the potluck Shannon brought peanuts M & M's mints and pretzels.

COMMAS TO SEPARATE ADJECTIVES

Use commas to separate two or more equally important adjectives.

Examples:
Alex avoided the **friendly, talkative, pleasant** boy sitting next to him at school.
The carpenter repaired the floor with **dark, aged, oak** flooring.
The reporter spoke with several **intense, talented** high school athletes.

Pay close attention to the last sentence above. You'll notice that the words *several, high,* and *school* are also adjectives modifying *athletes*. Not all adjectives modifying the same word are equally important. Only those of equal importance are separated with a comma. If you apply one or both of these tests, you can easily tell whether a comma is needed:

- Change the order of the adjectives. If the sentence reads just as clearly, separate the adjectives with a comma. If the sentence becomes unclear or sounds awkward, do not use a comma. The first two example sentences above make sense even if the position of the adjectives is changed. The last example sentence makes no sense if you change the order of any of the adjectives other than *intense* and *talented*. Therefore, those are the only adjectives separated by a comma.
  - ✓ Alex avoided the **talkative, friendly, pleasant** boy sitting next to him at school.
  - ✓ The carpenter repaired the floor with **aged, dark, oak** flooring.
  - ✗ The reporter spoke with **intense, several, high, talented, school** athletes.

- A second, equally effective test is to place *and* between the adjectives. If the sentence still reads well, then use commas between the adjectives. If the sentence sounds unclear or awkward, do not use commas. Again, this works with the first two example sentences, but in the last sentence, *and* makes sense only between *intense* and *talented*. Try these two tests with the following sentences. Where do commas go?
  We bought an **antique wrought iron** daybed.
  The envelope contained **three crisp clean brand new** hundred dollar bills.

You should have punctuated the sentences like this:

> We bought an **antique, wrought iron** daybed.
>
> The envelope contained **three crisp, clean, brand new** hundred dollar bills.

COMMAS TO SEPARATE OTHER ELEMENTS OF A SENTENCE

- Use commas to separate contrasting or opposing elements in a sentence. The comma functions as a signal to the reader: What follows is an opposite idea. It makes the idea easier for the reader to grasp.
  Examples:
  > We searched the entire house, **but found nothing**.
  >
  > We need strong intellects, **not strong bodies**, to resolve this problem.
  >
  > The racers ran slowly at first, **quickly at the end**.
  >
  > We expected to meet the President, **not a White House aide**.

- Use commas to separate words or phrases that interrupt the flow of thought in a sentence.
  Examples:
  > The deadline, **it seemed clear**, simply could not be met.
  >
  > We came to rely, **however**, on the kindness and generosity of the neighbors.
  >
  > The alternative route, **we discovered**, was faster than the original route.

- Whenever the name of the person being addressed is included in a sentence, it should be set off by commas.
  Examples:
  > **Dave**, we wanted you to look at this layout before we sent it to printing.
  >
  > We wanted you to look at this layout, **Dave**, before we sent it to printing.
  >
  > We wanted you to look at this layout before we sent it to printing, **Dave**.

- Mild exclamations included in a sentence are also set off with commas.
  Examples:
  > **Well**, that was certainly a pleasant surprise.
  >
  > **Yes**, I'll call you as soon as we get the information.
  >
  > **Heavens**, that was a long-winded speaker.

- Use a comma after the greeting and closing of a friendly letter.
  Examples:
  > Dear Uncle Jon,
  >
  > Sincerely yours,
  >
  > Yours truly,

PRACTICE

Choose the correctly punctuated version of each of the following sets of sentences. Keep in mind what you learned about commas in the previous lesson.

14. a. No, I haven't received a reply just yet, but I expect one any day.
    b. No I haven't received a reply just yet, but I expect one any day.
    c. No, I haven't received a reply just yet but I expect one any day.

15. a. My steak was burned to a crisp, the burger, on the other hand, was dripping with blood.
    b. My steak was burned to a crisp; the burger, on the other hand, was dripping with blood.
    c. My steak was burned to a crisp, the burger, on the other hand was dripping with blood.

16. a. Well, Sancha, I wonder if Mindy made it to her interview on time.
    b. Well, Sancha I wonder if Mindy made it to her interview on time.
    c. Well Sancha, I wonder if Mindy made it to her interview on time.

17. a. When we go on vacation, we need to remember our clothing fishing equipment and cameras.
    b. When we go on vacation we need to remember our clothing, fishing equipment, and cameras.
    c. When we go on vacation, we need to remember our clothing, fishing equipment, and cameras.

18. a. The correct address I believe is 215 North 34th, Streator, Illinois.
    b. The correct address, I believe, is 215 North 34th, Streator, Illinois.
    c. The correct address, I believe, is 215, North 34th, Streator, Illinois.

19. a. Our newest employee, a transfer from the home office, is the strong silent absent type, I think.
    b. Our newest employee, a transfer from the home office is the strong, silent, absent type, I think.
    c. Our newest employee, a transfer from the home office, is the strong, silent, absent type, I think.

20. a. I'm afraid, Mr. Dobbs, that you lack the qualifications for this job; but we have another that might interest you.
    b. I'm afraid Mr. Dobbs, that you lack the qualifications for this job, but we have another that might interest you.
    c. I'm afraid, Mr. Dobbs, that you lack the qualifications for this job, but we have another that might interest you.

21. a. Usually, at the company picnic we play badminton, frisbee golf, volleyball, and horseshoes.

    b. Usually, at the company picnic, we play badminton frisbee golf, volleyball and horseshoes.

    c. Usually, at the company picnic we play badminton, frisbee, golf, volleyball, and horseshoes.

22. a. We will advertise our biggest sale of the decade on June 21, 1997, the 25th anniversary of our Grand Opening sale.

    b. We will advertise our biggest sale of the decade on June 21 1997, the 25th anniversary of our Grand Opening sale.

    c. We will advertise our biggest sale of the decade on June 21, 1997 the 25th anniversary of our Grand Opening sale.

23. a. Exhausted by the heat, rather than the exertion, Ming collapsed under a tall shady oak tree.

    b. Exhausted by the heat rather than the exertion, Ming collapsed under a tall, shady oak tree.

    c. Exhausted by the heat, rather than the exertion, Ming collapsed under a tall, shady oak tree.

Skill Building Until Next Time

As you read the newspaper, a book or written materials at work or school, take special note of the commas you see. Try to remember why a comma might be used in each of the situations. Since commas are one of the most frequently misused punctuation marks, look for places where other writers have misused them.

ANSWERS

1. You can safely view an eclipse through the viewing glass of a welding helmet, or you can look through a piece of overexposed film.

2. The prisoner showed no remorse as the guilty verdict was announced, nor did the tears of the victim's family arouse any emotion.

3. The young calf put its head over the fence, and it licked my hand and sucked on my fingers.

4. Icebergs in the Antarctic are flat and smooth, but those in the Arctic are rough.

5. I understand your position on this issue; I still believe you are dead wrong.

6. I like Sam; he likes me, for we are best of friends.

7. The inventory is valued at one million dollars, but it's not enough to cover our debt.

8. If you know of anyone with data processing experience, encourage him or her to apply for this new position.

9. After he ran into the mayor's car with his truck, Adam used his cellular phone to call the police, his doctor, his lawyer, and his insurance agent.

10. The homegrown philosopher who lives next door at 251 Acorn Street, Libertyville, Kansas, claims to know exactly who invented the wheel, sliced bread, and kissing.

11. Estelle was born on January 31, 1953, and Arun was born on June 30, 1960.

12. Looking for a solution to the printing problem, Karissa asked an older employee, questioned the supervisor, and finally consulted the printer manual.

13. Baruch brought a jello salad to the potluck. Shannon brought peanuts, M & M's, mints, and pretzels.

14. a.
15. b.
16. a.
17. c.
18. b.
19. c.
20. c.
21. c.
22. a.
23. c.

L·E·S·S·O·N 6

SEMICOLONS AND COLONS

LESSON SUMMARY

Many people are confused by semicolons (;) and colons (:), but after you work through this lesson, you'll know exactly what to do with both of them.

You learned to use semicolons to separate independent clauses in Lesson 3. In this lesson you'll review that use of semicolons, as well as the use of some of the other punctuation marks you have studied so far. You will learn how to use semicolons with conjunctive adverbs and when to separate items in a series with semicolons. You will also learn to use colons in business communications and other settings.

Begin by seeing how much you know. Insert semicolons and colons where you think they are needed in the **Problem** column on the following page. Check yourself against the correct version in the **Solution** column on the right as you go.

Problem

Dear Mr. Powell

This letter is a formal complaint regarding service our company received from your representatives at 130 P.M. on January 26, 1996. These are the procedures for which we were billed a complete scotomy, a procedure to rid the machinery of electrostatic material a comprehensive assessment, a procedure for checking all mechanical and electronic parts in the machinery a thorough cleaning, a procedure necessary to keep the machine running efficiently.

This may be what the representative reported to have done however, only the first procedure in the list was finished. Only one of the three items was completed therefore, we should be refunded the amount charged for the other two services.

We are filing this complaint in accordance with your technical manual *McDounah New Age Electronics A Complete Manual*. This information is found in Volume 2, page 27 "Customers dissatisfied with our service for any reason have the right to file a full complaint within 10 (ten) days from the date of service. Such a complaint must be addressed in writing to Mr. Douglas Powell, Service Manager McDounah New Age Electronics Demming,

Solution

Dear Mr. Powell:

This letter is a formal complaint regarding service our company received from your representatives at 1:30 P.M. on January 26, 1996. These are the procedures for which we were billed: a complete scotomy, a procedure to rid the machinery of electrostatic material; a comprehensive assessment, a procedure for checking all mechanical and electronic parts in the machinery; a thorough cleaning, a procedure necessary to keep the machine running efficiently.

This may be what the representative reported to have done; however, only the first procedure in the list was finished. Only one of the three items was completed; therefore, we should be refunded the amount charged for the other two services.

We are filing this complaint in accordance with your technical manual *McDounah New Age Electronics: A Complete Manual*. This information is found in Volume 2, page 27: "Customers dissatisfied with our service for any reason have the right to file a full complaint within 10 (ten) days from the date of service. Such a complaint must be addressed in writing to Mr. Douglas Powell, Service Manager; McDounah New Age Electronics; Demming,

(continued on next page)

Problem (continued)

Delaware. Mr. Powell will respond within two days to remedy the alleged problem or to refund the amount in question."

We appreciate your prompt attention to this matter.

Sincerely yours,

Solution (continued)

Delaware. Mr. Powell will respond within two days to remedy the alleged problem or to refund the amount in question."

We appreciate your prompt attention to this matter.

Sincerely yours,

SEMICOLONS

There are three different cases in which a semicolon is used to separate independent clauses. (See Lesson 3 if you've forgotten what an independent clause is.)

- To separate independent clauses joined without a conjunction. This rule may seem familiar to you because it was also included in the last lesson.
  Examples:
    Three doctors began the research project; only one completed it.
    Discard the packaging; save the paperwork for accounting.
    The hour is over; it's time to stop working.
- To separate independent clauses that contain commas even if the clauses are joined by a conjunction. The semicolon helps the reader see where the break in thought occurs.
  Example:
    The team needed new equipment, updated training manuals, and better professional advice; but since
        none of this was provided, they performed as poorly as they had in the previous competition.
- To separate independent clauses connected with a conjunctive adverb. Follow the adverb with a comma. A *conjunctive adverb* is an adverb that joins independent clauses. Conjunctive adverbs are punctuated differently than regular conjunctions. The first independent clause is followed by a semicolon; the conjunctive adverb is followed by a comma.
  Examples:
    Our copy of the central warehouse catalog arrived after the budget deadline; **consequently,** our requests
        are late.
    In the book *An American Childhood,* Annie Dillard recounts her experiences as a child; **furthermore,** she
        questions and speculates about the meaning of life.

Here is a complete list of words used as conjunctive adverbs.

accordingly	furthermore	instead	otherwise
besides	hence	moreover	therefore
consequently	however	nevertheless	thus

Many people confuse subordinating conjunctions, such as *because, though, until,* and *while,* with the conjunctive adverbs listed above. The difference is important. A clause beginning with a subordinating conjunction is only a subordinate clause; it can't stand alone as a sentence. A clause with a conjunctive adverb is an *independent clause,* which should be separated from another independent clause with a period and capital letter or with a semicolon.

Here's a trick for finding out whether the word that begins a clause is a conjunctive adverb. If you can move the word around within the clause, it's a conjunctive adverb. If you can't, it's probably a subordinating conjunction. For example, here are two main clauses:

My paycheck was delayed. I couldn't pay my rent on time.

Here are two ways of joining those two main clauses:

My paycheck was delayed; therefore, I couldn't pay my rent on time.
I couldn't pay my rent on time because my paycheck was delayed.

Check whether the first version uses a conjunctive adverb. Can you move *therefore* around in its clause? Yes, you could say, "I couldn't, therefore, pay my rent on time." So *therefore* is a conjunctive adverb.

Use the same test to see whether *because* is a conjunctive adverb that should come after a semicolon. Can you move *because* around in its clause? "My paycheck because was delayed"? No. So *because* is a subordinating conjunction, and the clause it introduces is not a main clause.

There's one more way a semicolon is used to separate:

■ Use a semicolon to separate items in a series if the items contain commas. Unlike items in a series separated by commas, a semicolon is used even when there IS a conjunction.

Examples:

The dates we are considering for our annual party are Thursday, **June 5; Saturday, June 7; Sunday, June 8; or** Monday, June 9.

When we go to the lake, I am sure to take a pizza pan, a popcorn popper, and pancake **griddle; fishing** tackle, life jackets, and ski **equipment; and** puzzles, cards, board games, and my guitar.

The expansion committee is considering locations in Columbus, **Ohio; Orange, California; Minton, Tennessee; and** Jacksonville, Florida.

PRACTICE

Practice what you've learned by adding semicolons where they are needed in the following sentences. You will find the answers at the end of this lesson.

1. I need a break I've been working for five hours straight.

2. We have branch offices in Paris, France Berlin, Germany Stockholm, Sweden and Budapest, Hungary.

3. We had no problem meeting the deadline however, we were still able to find ways of streamlining production.

4. We ate swiss steak, riced potatoes, steamed broccoli and fresh bread for dinner but we still had room to eat apple pie for dessert.

5. Paige left some of the confidential documents sitting on her desk at work consequently, she worried about their safety all night long.

COLONS

COLONS THAT INTRODUCE

- Use a colon to introduce a list of items, as long as the part before the colon is already a complete sentence.
  Examples:
    These people were cast in the play: Andrea, Horatio, Thom, Alley and Benito.
    We packed these items for the trip: cameras, dress clothes, scuba equipment, and beach wear.
- Do not use a colon if the list of items complements a verb; in other words, if it completes the meaning begun by the verb. Look at the sample sentences from above rewritten in such a way that a colon is not necessary.
  Examples:
    The people cast in the play were Kristin, Horatio, Thom, Alley, and Benito.
    For our trip we packed cameras, dress clothes, scuba equipment, and beach wear.
- Use a colon to introduce a formal quotation.
  Example:
    John F. Kennedy ended the speech with these notable words: "Ask not what your country can do for you. Ask what you can do for your country."

- Use a colon to emphasize a word, phrase, or clause that adds particular emphasis to the main body of a sentence. Again, the part before the colon should already be a complete sentence.

    Example:

    > The financial problems our company has been experiencing have been caused by one thing: poor planning.
    >
    > We were missing a vital piece of information: how the basic product design differed from last year's model.

COLONS THAT SHOW A SUBORDINATE RELATIONSHIP

Use a colon to show a subordinate relationship in the following cases:

- Between two sentences when the second explains the first.

    Examples:

    > Brenton shouted and threw his fists in the air: He had just set a new world's record.
    >
    > Nicole put the check into her scrapbook rather than cashing it: It was the first check she had ever earned.
    >
    > Scott ignored the phone: He knew it was a salesman for whom he had no time.

- Between the title and the subtitle of a book.

    Examples:

    > *Internet Starter Kit: A Complete Guide to Cyberspace*
    >
    > *Beyond 2000: A Futuristic View of Time*
    >
    > *O Death, Where is Thy Sting: Tales from the Other Side*

- Between volume and page number or between chapter and verse.

    Examples:

    > *World Book Encyclopedia* V: 128
    >
    > *New Age Journal of Medicine* IX: 23
    >
    > John 3:16
    >
    > Genesis 1:1
    >
    > Psalms 23:2

- Between hour and minute.

    Examples:

    > 12:53 A.M.
    >
    > 2:10 P.M.

- After the greeting of a business letter. You learned that commas are used after greetings in personal or friendly letters. A colon signals the reader that what is to follow is a business matter, something to be taken seriously. This is particularly true if you include the position, but not the name of the person to whom the letter is addressed. However, even in a business letter, the closing is followed by a comma.

    Examples:

    > Dear Mr. Strange:
    >
    > Cordially yours,
    >
    > Dear Operations Manager:
    >
    > Respectfully submitted,

PRACTICE

Choose the correctly punctuated version in each of the following sets of sentences. You will find the correct answers at the end of the lesson.

6. a. I found an outline of the procedure in the policy manual, Volume 3: 17.
   b. I found an outline of the procedure, in the policy manual, Volume 3: 17.
   c. I found an outline of the procedure in the policy manual Volume 3, 17.

7. a. The tornado destroyed most of the buildings on our farm, however the house was untouched by the violent storm.
   b. The tornado destroyed most of the buildings on our farm; however the house was untouched by the violent storm.
   c. The tornado destroyed most of the buildings on our farm; however, the house was untouched by the violent storm.

8. a. After a week in the woods I need: a towel, a washcloth, a toothbrush, and a bar of soap.
   b. After a week in the woods I need a towel, a washcloth, a toothbrush, and a bar of soap.
   c. After a week in the woods I need; a towel, a washcloth, a toothbrush, and a bar of soap.

9. a. Dear Subscriber,
      Please renew your subscription by 12,00 A.M. on January 5, 1996, to receive the special bonus.
   b. Dear Subscriber:
      Please renew your subscription by 12:00 A.M. on January 5, 1996, to receive the special bonus.
   c. Dear Subscriber;
      Please renew your subscription by 12:00 A.M. on January 5, 1996 to receive the special bonus.

10. a. Each day a new shift begins at 8:00 A.M., 4:00 P.M., and 12:00 A.M.
   b. Each day a new shift begins at 8:00 A.M.; 4:00 P.M.; and 12:00 A.M.
   c. Each day a new shift begins at 8:00, A.M.; 4:00, P.M.; and 12:00, A.M.

11. a. I like to play football, a physically challenging sport; chess, a game of logic and strategy; Super Mario World, a mindless Super Nintendo game; and the guitar, a relaxing instrument.
   b. I like to play football, a physically challenging sport: chess, a game of logic and strategy: Super Mario World, a mindless Super Nintendo game: and the guitar, a relaxing instrument.
   c. I like to play football a physically challenging sport, chess a game of logic and strategy, Super Mario World a mindless Super Nintendo game, and the guitar a relaxing instrument.

12. a. They learned the following information from the interrogation: the suspect's name; the suspect's home address; the suspect's phone number; and the suspect's current employer.

b. They learned the following information from the interrogation the suspect's name, the suspect's home address, the suspect's phone number, and the suspect's current employer.

c. They learned the following information from the interrogation: the suspect's name, the suspect's home address, the suspect's phone number, and the suspect's current employer.

Skill Building Until Next Time

Take a look at some of the letters or communications you have received or written recently. Examine the punctuation. Did the author use endmarks, commas, semicolons and colons correctly? If not, correct them. It will be good practice.

ANSWERS

1. I need a break; I've been working for five hours straight.
2. We have branch offices in Paris, France; Berlin, Germany; Stockholm, Sweden; and Budapest, Hungary.
3. We had no problem meeting the deadline; however, we were still able to find ways of streamlining production.
4. We ate swiss steak, riced potatoes, steamed broccoli and fresh bread for dinner; but we still had room to eat apple pie for dessert.
5. Paige left some of the confidential documents sitting on her desk at work; consequently, she worried about their safety all night long.
6. a.
7. c.
8. b.
9. b.
10. a.
11. a.
12. c.

L·E·S·S·O·N 7

APOSTROPHES AND DASHES

LESSON SUMMARY

This lesson will put you in control of apostrophes (') and dashes (—), two of the most commonly misused marks of punctuation.

A postrophes communicate important information in written language. Dashes, when used sparingly, add emphasis. Before you begin the lesson, see how much you already know. Add apostrophes—and one pair of dashes—where you think they belong in the **Problem** column on the following page. Check yourself with the **Solution** column.

Problem

My grandfather is quite fond of telling stories from the late 30s and early 40s. The Great Depressions effect was beginning to diminish in the small South Dakota town where he lived. He inherited a 160-acre farm after his father-in-laws death in 1938. Little of the farms cropland had produced anything in the years prior to 38. During his first two years as a landowner, he netted a small profit. With the droughts end in 40 came the beginning of good crops. Even with the governments market quotas, he was able to make enough money to buy another quarter of land. He counted on his sons help to farm the addl land, but they went off to Europe when World War II broke out. He purchased a steam engine tractor one of John Deeres first and farmed the 320 acres by himself. That was the beginning of his most successful years as a farmer.

Solution

My grandfather is quite fond of telling stories from the late '30s and early '40s. The Great Depression's effect was beginning to diminish in the small South Dakota town where he lived. He inherited a 160-acre farm after his father-in-law's death in 1938. Little of the farm's cropland had produced anything in the years prior to '38. During his first two years as a landowner, he netted a small profit. With the drought's end in '40 came the beginning of good crops. Even with the government's market quotas, he was able to make enough money to buy another quarter of land. He counted on his sons' help to farm the add'l land, but they went off to Europe when World War II broke out. He purchased a steam engine tractor—one of John Deere's first—and farmed the 320 acres by himself. That was the beginning of his most successful years as a farmer.

APOSTROPHES

TO SHOW POSSESSION

Use an apostrophe to show possession. The highlighted words in each of the following examples are *possessive adjectives*: They show to whom or what a noun belongs.

Singular nouns (add *'s*)	Plural nouns ending in *s* (add *'*)	Plural nouns not ending in *s*
boy's toy (The toy is the **boy's**.)	**boys'** bicycles (The bicycles are the **boys'**.)	**men's** schedules (The schedules are the **men's**.)
child's play	**kids'** bedrooms	**children's** opinions
lady's coat	**ladies'** skirts	**women's** department
dentist's aide	**players'** representative	**people's** choice

Apostrophes are *not* used to form plurals. When you're thinking of putting an apostrophe in a noun that ends in *s*, ask yourself whether you're merely showing that there's more than one thing. If so, there's no apostrophe.

Examples:
There are a lot of **potatoes** in the refrigerator.
Cut out the **potatoes'** eyes.

You can avoid putting apostrophes in words that are merely plurals by trying this formula: *the _____ of the _____*, as in *the eyes of the potatoes*. If the words don't fit in that formula, the noun doesn't take an apostrophe. Here are some special cases for the use of apostrophes to show possession.

- When there is more than one word in the possessive adjective—for example, with a compound noun, a business or institution, or jointly possessed items—add the apostrophe *s* to the last word of the compound.
  Examples:
  someone **else's** problem
  mother-in-**law's** visit
  board of **directors'** policy
  Pope John Paul **II's** illness
  Proctor and **Gamble's** product
  Wayne and **Judy's** log cabin
- Words showing periods of time or amounts of money need apostrophes when they are used as possessive adjectives.
  Examples:
  day's pay, **month's** vacation, **morning's** work
  two **cents'** worth, **dollar's** worth
- A singular noun that ends in *s* still takes apostrophe *s*, though some writers omit the *s* and include only the apostrophe.
  Examples:
  Roger **Maris's** batting record
  Lotus's personal organizer
- With a possessive pronoun (*my, mine, our, ours, your, yours, his, her, hers, their, theirs*) is used as an adjective, no apostrophe is needed.
  Examples:
  This is **their** idea. The idea is **theirs**.
  We filed **our** flight plan. The flight plan is **ours**.
  This manual must be **yours**.

PRACTICE

From each set below, choose the option in which apostrophes are used correctly. You will find the answers to each set of questions at the end of the lesson.

1. a. An employee's motivation is different from an owner's.
   b. An employees' motivation is different from an owners'.

2. a. Employees reward's differ from an owners'.
   b. Employees' rewards differ from an owner's.

3. a. Elaine has worked three years as a physicians assistant.
   b. Elaine has worked three years as a physician's assistant.

4. a. The Mens' Issue's group meets every Saturday morning.
   b. The Men's Issues group meets every Saturday morning.

5. a. The companies' sales force has doubled in recent years, and the credit is your's.
   b. The company's sales force has doubled in recent years, and the credit is yours.

6. a. The most efficient method is her's.
   b. The most efficient method is hers.

7. a. After five years' experience, we earn four weeks' paid vacation.
   b. After five year's experience, we earn four week's paid vacation.

8. a. Pat and Janice's proposal requires a month's work.
   b. Pat's and Janice's proposal requires a months' work.

9. a. The computer supply store's top-selling printer is Hewlett Packards latest model.
   b. The computer supply store's top-selling printer is Hewlett Packard's latest model.

10. a. Ms. Jones's boutique sells the same products as Mr. Smith's.
    b. Ms. Jones' boutique sells the same products as Mr. Smiths'.

TO SHOW OMISSION

Use an apostrophe to show that letters or numbers have been omitted.

Examples:

Morton **doesn't** (does not) live here anymore.

The officer **couldn't** (could not) give me a speeding ticket.

Who's (who is) on first?

I just **can't** (cannot) understand this memo.

The task force discussed the **nat'l** (national) debt.

My first car was a **'67** (1967) Chevy.

Grandpa tells stories about life in the **'40s** (1940s).

DASHES

A dash is a very specialized punctuation mark reserved for only a few special situations. However, many writers use it incorrectly in place of other marks. Dashes call attention to themselves. A careful writer uses them sparingly. Dashes are very effective if used correctly, but they lose their impact if they are overused.

Remember to distinguish a dash from a hyphen when typing. A dash is **two** hyphens.

- Use a dash to mark a sudden break in thought or to insert a comment.

  Examples:

  Here is your sandwich and your—Look out for that bee!

  I remember the day—what middle-aged person doesn't—that President Kennedy was shot.

  John is sorry—we all are—about your unfortunate accident.

- Use a dash to emphasize explanatory material. You don't have to use a dash, but you may.

  Examples:

  Knowing yourself—your thoughts, values, and dreams—is the most important knowledge.

  "The writer is by nature a dreamer—a conscious dreamer." —*Carson McCullers*

  We spend our summers in Canada—Ontario, to be precise.

- Use a dash to indicate omitted letters or words.

  Examples:

  "Oh, sh—, I can't believe I forgot to mail that package!"

  "Hello?—Yes, I can hear you just fine.—Of course—I think I can.—Good!—I'll see you later.—

- Use a dash to connect a beginning phrase to the rest of the sentence.

  Examples:

  Honesty, integrity, tenacity—these are marks of motivated salespeople.

  Nashville, Tennessee; Olympia, Washington; Oceola, Iowa—these are the prospective locations.

PRACTICE

Choose the option in which dashes and other punctuation are used correctly in each of the following sets.

11. a. We have only one choice—to open a new branch office in the suburbs.
    b. We have only one choice to open a new branch office—in the suburbs.

12. a. My suggestion—just in case you're interested, is to apply for a promotion.
    b. My suggestion—just in case you're interested—is to apply for a promotion.

13. a. He is the most unreasonable, I guess I should keep my opinions to myself.
    b. He is the most unreasonable—I guess I should keep my opinions to myself.

14. a. I can't find that d— pocket organizer that I worked—Oh, here it is.
    b. I can't find that d— pocket organizer that I worked, Oh, here it is.

15. a. Brains, brawn, determination—that's what I demand from my people.
    b. Brains, brawn, determination: that's what I demand from my people.

PRACTICE AND REVIEW

Check yourself with these sample test questions. These extremely difficult questions cover much of what you have learned about punctuation so far. Look at the items carefully. Which of the following options is punctuated correctly?

16. a. Although it may seem strange, my partners purpose in interviewing Dr. E. S. Sanders Jr., was to eliminate him as a suspect in the crime.
    b. Although it may seem strange my partner's purpose in interviewing Dr. E. S. Sanders, Jr. was to eliminate him, as a suspect in the crime.
    c. Although it may seem strange, my partner's purpose in interviewing Dr. E. S. Sanders, Jr., was to eliminate him as a suspect in the crime.
    d. Although it may seem strange, my partner's purpose in interviewing Dr. E. S. Sanders, Jr. was to eliminate him, as a suspect in the crime.

17. a. After colliding with a vehicle at the intersection of Grand, and Forest Ms. Anderson saw a dark hooded figure reach through the window, grab a small parcel and run north on Forest.

b. After colliding with a vehicle at the intersection of Grand, and Forest, Ms. Anderson saw a dark hooded figure reach through the window, grab a small parcel, and run north on Forest.

c. After colliding with a vehicle at the intersection of Grand and Forest Ms. Anderson saw a dark, hooded figure reach through the window, grab a small parcel and run north on Forest.

d. After colliding with a vehicle at the intersection of Grand and Forest, Ms. Anderson saw a dark, hooded figure reach through the window, grab a small parcel, and run north on Forest.

18. a. When we interviewed each of the boys and the fathers, we determined that the men's stories did not match up with the boy's versions.

b. When we interviewed each of the boys and the fathers, we determined that the men's stories did not match up with the boys' versions.

c. When we interviewed each of the boys and the fathers, we determined that the mens' stories did not match up with the boys' versions.

d. When we interviewed each of the boy's and the father's, we determined that the men's stories did not match up with the boys' versions.

19. a. Bring these items when you drive up here tomorrow—Bobbys sleeping bag, another can of insect repellent, the girls queen-sized air mattress—they want to use it to sunbathe on the water, and my swimming trunks.

b. Bring these items when you drive up here tomorrow: Bobby's sleeping bag, another can of insect repellent, the girls' queen-sized air mattress—they want to use it to sunbathe on the water—and my swimming trunks.

c. Bring these items when you drive up here tomorrow: Bobby's sleeping bag, another can of insect repellent, the girl's queen-sized air mattress—they want to use it to sunbathe on the water, and my swimming trunks.

d. Bring these items when you drive up here tomorrow. Bobby's sleeping bag, another can of insect repellent, the girls queen-sized air mattress, they want to use it to sunbathe on the water, and my swimming trunks.

20. a. James Autry, Steven Covey, Madeline Hunter—these authors are responsible for my management style, a combination of Autry's personnel philosophy, Covey's process for prioritizing, and Hunter's organizational principles.

   b. James Autry, Steven Covey, Madeline Hunter. These authors are responsible for my management style, a combination of Autry's personnel philosophy, Covey's process for prioritizing and Hunter's organizational principles.

   c. James Autry, Steven Covey, Madeline Hunter—these authors are responsible for my management style, a combination of Autrys personnel philosophy, Coveys process for prioritizing and Hunters organizational principles.

   d. James Autry, Steven Covey, Madeline Hunter: these authors are responsible for my management style; a combination of Autry's personnel philosophy; Covey's process for prioritizing; and Hunter's organizational principles.

Skill Building Until Next Time

Few people understand the rules of apostrophes and dashes fully. Advertisers are notorious for misusing both types of punctuation. Pay special attention to billboards and advertisements in newspapers and magazines. Look for places where apostrophes and dashes are used correctly. Notice places where they are omitted or added when they shouldn't be. If your school or job produces promotional material, examine some of your own literature to see if apostrophes and dashes have been used correctly.

ANSWERS

1. a.	**6.** b.	**11.** a.	**16.** c.
2. b.	**7.** a.	**12.** b.	**17.** d.
3. b.	**8.** a.	**13.** b.	**18.** b.
4. b.	**9.** b.	**14.** a.	**19.** b.
5. b.	**10.** a.	**15.** a.	**20.** a.

L·E·S·S·O·N

QUOTATION MARKS

8

LESSON SUMMARY

This lesson covers rules regarding the use of quotation marks, both double and single. Although these marks are most often found in dialogue, they are important in other writing situations as well.

Begin this lesson by seeing how much you already know about quotation marks. Insert them where you think they belong in the sentences in the **Problem** column on the following page. Some sentences will also need endmarks and commas. Check yourself against the corrected versions of the sentences in the **Solution** column.

Problem	**Solution**
Into the shelter yelled the captain.	"Into the shelter!" yelled the captain.
My first personal essay was called My Life and Death.	My first personal essay was called "My Life and Death."
William Hickock richly deserved the name Wild Bill.	William Hickock richly deserved the name "Wild Bill."
I wish that old fussbudget— Melanie stopped abruptly as Mr. Harris walked into the room.	"I wish that old fussbudget—" Melanie stopped abruptly as Mr. Harris walked into the room.
None of us had heard of halupsi before.	None of us had heard of "halupsi" before.
If we don't hurry said Jack we'll be late for the show.	"If we don't hurry," said Jack, "we'll be late for the show."
Why are you still here my supervisor asked. Everyone else went home an hour ago.	"Why are you still here?" my supervisor asked. "Everyone else went home an hour ago."
I read the editorial called Big Boys in Washington.	I read the editorial called "Big Boys in Washington."
You've said actually twelve times in the past two minutes.	You've said "actually" twelve times in the past two minutes.
David said The customer said No way before I ever had a chance to explain.	David said, "The customer said, 'No way!' before I ever had a chance to explain."
We matted and framed a print of Woodland Tide and hung it on the office wall.	We matted and framed a print of "Woodland Tide" and hung it on the office wall.
Our Christmas bonus was a bag with a cookie and an orange.	Our Christmas "bonus" was a bag with a cookie and an orange.
With his tardy record, I can see why you refer to him as Punctual Paul.	With his tardy record, I can see why you refer to him as "Punctual Paul."

QUOTATION MARKS WITH DIRECT QUOTATIONS

- Use quotation marks to set off a direct quotation or thought within a sentence or paragraph. This includes quotations that are signed, etched, inscribed, carved, and so on.

  Examples:

  Mr. Hurley called our prototype "a model of pure genius."

  I was certain he said, "Campbells will accept delivery on Tuesday."

  "When will help arrive?" I wondered.

  The sign clearly read, "No trespassing or hunting."

  "Happy and Fulfilled," the headstone read.

- Do *not* use quotation marks for paraphrases or indirect quotations.

  Examples:

  I was sure Campbells wanted a Tuesday delivery.

  I wondered when help would arrive.

  The sign said that trespassing and hunting were not allowed.

- Use single quotation marks to set off a quotation within a quotation.

  Examples:

  "I distinctly heard her say, 'The store opens at 9:00.'" said Gene.

  The speaker continued, "I am ever mindful of Franklin Roosevelt's famous words, 'We have nothing to fear but fear itself.' But fear is a terrible thing."

  My speech teacher asked, "Does anyone in this room remember the way Jim Nabors used to say, 'Golly'?"

A WORD ABOUT DIALOGUE

Correctly punctuating dialogue means understanding how to use quotation marks, commas, and endmarks. Take a close look at the sentences in the dialogue sample below. They include the basic dialogue structures. The words quoted are called *quotations*, and the words explaining who said the quotations are called *tags*. In the sample below, the tags are highlighted.

1. "I'm really thirsty. Let's grab something to drink," **said Horace.**

2. **Nancy replied,** "I'm thirsty, but I don't have any cash. Do you have some?"

3. "I don't get it," **Horace answered.** "You're the manager with the high-paying job."

4. "Well," **Nancy replied,** "credit cards are all I ever use."

Quoted words are always surrounded by quotation marks. Place quotation marks before a group of quoted words and again at the end.

Tags are punctuated differently depending upon where they appear in the sentence. Whenever the tag follows a quotation, and the quotation is a sentence that would normally be punctuated with a period, use a comma at the end of the quotation. The period comes at the end of the tag. However, if the quotation is a sentence that would normally be followed with a question mark or an exclamation point, insert the question mark or exclamation point at the end of the quotation. Place a period after the tag. (See sentence 1 on page 73.)

> "I'm really thirsty. Let's grab something to drink," said Alvina.
>
> "I'm really thirsty. Do you want to grab something to drink?" asked Alvina.
>
> "I'm really thirsty. Hold it—a Dairy Queen!" exclaimed Alvina.

Sometimes, the tag precedes the quotation. When this happens, place a comma after the tag. Put quotation marks around the quoted words, capitalize the first word of the quotation, and punctuate the sentence as you would normally. (See sentence 2 on page 73.)

Sometimes, the tag interrupts the quotation. If both the first and second parts of the quotation are complete sentences, the first part of the quotation is punctuated in the same way as a quotation with the tag at the end. In other words, the period follows the tag. The rest of the quotation is punctuated in the same way as a quotation preceded by a tag. (See sentence 3 on page 73.)

When the tag interrupts the quotation and the sentence, the words preceding the tag begin the thought, and the words following the tag complete the thought. Place quotation marks around the quoted words and follow the first part of the quotation with a comma. Place a comma after the tag (not a period, since the sentence is not completed). Place quotation marks around the last part of the quotation, but **do not** capitalize the first letter of the quotation. It is not the beginning of a sentence. Punctuate the rest of the sentence as you would normally. (See sentence 4 on page 73.)

NOTICE: All of the punctuation is **inside** the quotation marks except the punctuation marks following the tags.

Dialogue at a Glance

- Tag following the quotation mark:

    "————," said Rose.

    "————?" asked Rose.

    "————!" exclaimed Rose.

- Tag preceding quotation:

    Iris said, "————."

    Iris asked, "————?"

    Iris exclaimed, "————!"

- Tag between two sentences of a quotation:

    "————," said Lily. "————."

    "————?" asked Lily. "————?"

    "————!" exclaimed Lily. "————!"

- Tag interrupting a quotation and a sentence:

    "————," said Daisy, "————."

    "————," asked Daisy, "————?"

    "————," exclaimed Daisy, "————!"

OTHER USES OF QUOTATION MARKS

- Use quotation marks to set off unfamiliar terms and nicknames. Quotation marks are sometimes used to refer to words used as words, though you will often see italics for words used as words.

    Examples:

    None of us had heard of "chutney" before we read the article.

    He was dubbed "Sir Tagalong" by the other members of the staff.

    The Scrabble players disagreed over the term "ptu." (or " . . . over the term *ptu*.")

- Use quotation marks to indicate irony or raised eyebrows. But avoid overusing quotation marks in this way; it doesn't work if you do it all the time.

    Examples:

    When we were camping, our "bathroom" was a thicket behind our tent.

    Our "guide" never mentioned the presence of poison ivy.

    The "fun" of surgery begins long before the operation commences.

- Use quotation marks to set off titles of certain items. Other titles should be underlined or italicized.

Enclose in quotation marks	Underline or italicize
name of a short story or chapter of a book	title of a novel
name of a T.V. program	name of a movie
title of a poem	title of a collection of poetry or an epic poem
headline of an article or title of a report	name of a magazine or newspaper
title of a song	title of a musical, play, or long musical composition
	name of a ship, plane, train, etc.

PUNCTUATING WITHIN QUOTATION MARKS

Here are the rules regarding the use of other punctuation marks and quotation marks.

- Question marks, exclamation points, and dashes go inside the quotation marks if they are part of the quotation. If they are not, place them outside the quotation marks.

Examples:

The doctor asked, "Can you feel any pain in this area?" [Part of the quotation]

Have you read Nathaniel Hawthorne's "The Birthmark"? [Not part of the quotation]

"I wish I'd never heard of—" Karen stopped abruptly as Nick walked in the room. [Part of the quotation]

"Stage left," "stage right," "upstage," and "downstage"—I always confused these terms. [Not part of the quotation]

- Periods and commas go **inside** closing quotation marks.

"Let's wait a few minutes," suggested Doris, "before we leave."

- Colons and semicolons go **outside** closing quotation marks.

I can see only one challenge for the speaker of "The Road Less Traveled": ambivalence.

The critic called the latest sculpture an "abomination to sensitive eyes"; the artist was hurt.

PRACTICE

Choose the correctly punctuated version in each of the following sets of sentences. Check for punctuation other than quotation marks also.

1. a. "Have you ever read the story 'The Open Window' by O. Henry? asked Martha.
b. "Have you ever read the story 'The Open Window' by O. Henry?" asked Martha.
c. "Have you ever read the story "The Open Window" by O. Henry?" asked Martha.

2. a. Did you know it was Winston Churchill who called Russia "a riddle wrapped up in a mystery inside an enigma"?
b. Did you know it was "Winston Churchill" who called Russia "a riddle wrapped up in a mystery inside an enigma?"
c. Did you know it was Winston Churchill who called Russia "a riddle wrapped up in a mystery inside an enigma?"

3. a. After reading a review of Toy Story, I wanted to see the movie.
b. After reading a review of <u>Toy Story</u>, I wanted to see the movie.
c. After reading a review of "Toy Story," I wanted to see the movie.

4. a. Leaving five minutes early on Friday was our "reward."
b. Leaving five minutes early on Friday was our "reward".
c. Leaving five minutes early on Friday was our 'reward.'

5. a. "Megabyte," "baud speed," "internal RAM"—these are all examples of technical terms.
b. "Megabyte," "baud speed," "internal RAM—" these are all examples of technical terms.
c. "Megabyte", "baud speed", "internal RAM"—these are all examples of technical terms.

6. a. If you read my article Budget Play in this morning's <u>Register</u>, you'll understand why I'm so cynical about Washington politicians.

b. If you read my article "Budget Play" in this morning's "Register", you'll understand why I'm so cynical about Washington politicians.

c. If you read my article "Budget Play" in this morning's <u>Register</u>, you'll understand why I'm so cynical about Washington politicians.

7. a. "The story 'What Does Anyone Really Understand?' certainly gave me something to think about," remarked Uncle Art.

b. 'The story "What Does Anyone Really Understand?" certainly gave me something to think about,' remarked Uncle Art.

c. "The story "What Does Anyone Really Understand?" certainly gave me something to think about," remarked Uncle Art.

8. a. "Do you name all your cats Howard," asked my friend Ted.

b. "Do you name all your cats Howard"? asked my friend Ted.

c. "Do you name all your cats Howard?" asked my friend Ted.

9. a. The officer asked us whether we had seen the accident.

b. The officer asked us whether we had seen the accident?

c. The officer asked us, "Whether we had seen the accident."

10. a. "You would be better off not to offer any excuses," the personnel director advised, "I'm afraid that will only make matters worse."

b. "You would be better off not to offer any excuses." the personnel director advised. "I'm afraid that will only make matters worse."

c. "You would be better off not to offer any excuses," the personnel director advised. "I'm afraid that will only make matters worse."

Skill Building Until Next Time

Look for examples of quotation marks in anything you read. When you find them, check to see if they've been used correctly.

ANSWERS

1. b.
2. a.
3. b.
4. a.
5. a.

6. c.
7. a.
8. c.
9. a.
10. c.

L·E·S·S·O·N

"DESIGNER" PUNCTUATION

LESSON SUMMARY

This lesson covers some of the less commonly used punctuation marks, including hyphens, parentheses, brackets, ellipses, and diagonal slashes. While these marks aren't necessary all that often, when they *are* necessary it's important to use them correctly.

The punctuation marks covered in this lesson—hyphens, parentheses, brackets, ellipses, and diagonals—are not often used in regular writing. However, they serve very specific purposes. Knowing and understanding their functions gives a writer an advantage in communicating ideas. Since most of these rules are so specialized that few people know them, we'll begin immediately with the lesson rather than with an assessment of your current knowledge. The last part of the lesson discusses using numbers in written text.

HYPHENS

The main purpose of a hyphen (-) is to join words in creating compound nouns or adjectives. Hyphens signal words that work together for a single purpose.

Compound nouns may be written as a single word, as two words, or as a hyphenated word. Whenever you are in doubt, consult a recent dictionary. Since language changes constantly, these words also evolve. A compound noun written as two words may come to be written as a hyphenated word and eventually become a single word. For example, the word *semicolon* began as two separate words: *semi colon*. In the late 1950s, dictionaries began listing it as a hyphenated word: *semi-colon*. A recent dictionary will list it as a single word: *semicolon*.

Single-word compound nouns	Two-word compound nouns	Hyphenated compound nouns
tablecloth	parking lot	jack-in-the-box
horsefly	couch potato	brother-in-law
textbook	floppy disk	money-maker
catwalk		city-state
bedroom		well-being
		merry-go-round

- Use a hyphen to join two coequal nouns working together as one.
  Shannon is a **teacher-poet.**
  Pete Rose was a **player-coach** for the Cincinnati Reds.
  Kevin Costner has joined the ranks of well-known **actor-directors**.
- Use a hyphen to join multi-word compound nouns.
  fly-by-night, stick-in-the-mud, good-for-nothing, three-year-old
- Use a hyphen to join two or more words that function as a single adjective *preceding* the noun.
  The hikers saw a **run-down** cabin in the clearing.
  Much has been written about the **Kennedy-Nixon** debates.
  An **ill-trained** police officer is more of a menace than protector.
  The company employed a **high-powered** consultant.
  A **soft-spoken** answer to the angry accusation ended the disagreement.
  His **off-the-wall** remarks keep our meetings lively and interesting.
  The parties finally agreed after three months of **hard-nosed** negotiations.
  A **French-Canadian** bicyclist won the **three-week** race.
- If the words functioning as a single adjective *follow* the noun, they are not hyphenated.
  The cabin the hikers saw in the clearing was **run down.**
  A police officer who is **ill trained** is more of a menace than a protector.
  The consultant employed by the company was **high powered.**
  The parties finally agreed after three months of negotiations that were **hard nosed**.
- Use a hyphen to join prefixes such as *self, half, ex, all, great, post, pro,* and *vice,* or the suffix *elect,* to words.
  Harry Truman unleashed the **all-powerful** atomic weapon.
  Abraham Lincoln was a **self-made** man.
  Keep your **half-baked** ideas to yourself.

Simone spotted her **ex-husband** walking into the grocery store.

My **great-grandfather** turns 102 next Wednesday.

Many remember the **post-WWII** years with great fondness.

Conservatives consider the front-runner to be a **pro-abortion** candidate.

The **secretary-elect** picked up all the records from the presiding secretary.

- Use a hyphen to avoid confusing or awkward spellings.

    The coach decided to **re-pair** [rather than repair] the debate partners.

    The neighbors decided to **re-cover** [rather than recover] their old sofa.

    The sculpture had a **bell-like** [rather than belllike] shape.

- Use a hyphen to join a capital letter to a word.

    The **U-joint** went out in our second car.

    The architect worked with nothing more than a **T-square**.

- Use a hyphen to write two-word numbers between 21 and 99 as words.

    twenty-six, thirty-three, sixty-four, seventy-two, ninety-nine

- Use a hyphen to join fractions written as words.

    three-fifths, five-sixteenths, five thirty-seconds

- Use a hyphen to join numbers to words used as a single adjective.

    three-yard pass, eight-inch steel, two-word sentence, five-stroke lead

NOTE: When a series of similar number-word adjectives is written in a sentence, use a hyphen/comma combination with all but the last item in the series.

    Precut particle board comes in **two-, four-,** and **six-foot** squares.

    Andy scored three touchdowns on **eight-, fourteen-,** and **two-yard** runs.

- Use a hyphen to join numbers and adjectives.

    fifty-four-year-old woman, ten-dollar profit, two-thousand-acre ranch, twenty-minute wait

- Use a hyphen to write the time of day as words.

    twelve-thirty, four-o'clock appointment, six-fifteen A.M., one-fifty-five in the morning

- Use a hyphen to join numbers indicating a life span, a score, or the duration of an event.

    Abraham Lincoln (**1809-65**) served as the sixteenth President, **1861-65**.

    The Cowboys beat the Eagles **21-3**.

- Use a hyphen to separate a word between syllables at the end of a line. Here are a few guidelines for dividing words.

    Never leave a single-letter syllable on a line.

    Divide hyphenated words at the hyphen.

    Never divide a one-syllable word.

    Avoid dividing words that have fewer than six letters.

    Avoid dividing the last word of a paragraph.

    Avoid dividing a number.

    ALWAYS CHECK A DICTIONARY IF YOU ARE IN DOUBT.

PARENTHESES

- Use parentheses to enclose explanatory material that interrupts the normal flow of the sentences and is only marginally related to the text.

    Thirty-sixth Street (a party street if there ever was one) is a fun place to live.

    Our neighbors threw a huge party on New Year's Eve. (Fortunately, we were invited.)

    Unfortunately, another set of neighbors (they were not invited) called the police to complain about the noise.

    We party-goers (how were we to know?) were completely surprised by the officers.

Notice the last three sentences. Each set of parentheses contains a complete sentence. If the parenthetical construction comes at the end of a sentence, it is punctuated as its own sentence within the parentheses. On the other hand, if it comes within another sentence, no capital letters or periods are necessary. However, if the parenthetical construction in the middle of another sentence is a sentence that would normally require a question mark or exclamation point, include that punctuation.

- Use parentheses to enclose information when accuracy is essential.

    The two sons of Richard Hannika (Scott and William) are sole heirs to his fortune.

    We hereby agree to sell the heirloom for sixty-three dollars ($63.00).

- Use parentheses to enclose letters or numbers marking a division.

    This lesson includes several little-used, often-misused punctuation marks: (a) hyphens, (b) parentheses, (c) brackets, (d) diagonals, and (e) ellipses.

    Your task consists of three steps: (1) locating information, (2) writing a report, and (3) delivering a presentation about your findings.

BRACKETS

- Use brackets to enclose parenthetical material within parentheses.

    Brandi planned to work as an aeronautic engineer (she completed an internship at National Aeronautics and Space Administration [NASA]) as soon as she completed her doctoral work.

- Use brackets to enclose words inserted into a quotation.

    "The next head nurse [Shawna DeWitt] will face the challenge of operating the floor with a reduced staff."

- Use brackets around the word *sic* to show that an error in a quotation was made by the original writer or speaker.

    "Unless we heel [sic] the nation's economic woes, social problems will continue to mount."

ELLIPSES

Points of ellipsis look like periods, but they do not function as endmarks. Type three periods to form ellipses. These marks indicate omitted material or long pauses.

- Use ellipses to show that quoted material has been omitted. If the omission comes at the end of a sentence, follow the ellipses with a period.

    "Four-score and seven years ago… equal."

    "We hold these truths to be self-evident…."
- Use ellipses to indicate a pause or hesitation.

    And the winner for "Best Actor" is… Dustin Hoffman.

    I think that adds up to… exactly eighty-three dollars.

DIAGONALS

Much like the hyphen, a diagonal is a mark used to join words or numbers. The most frequent use of the diagonal is with the phrase *and/or*, which shows that the sentence refers to one or both of the words being joined.

    For breakfast we can make bacon and/or French toast.

    Vinegar and/or egg whites added to plain water will make an excellent hair rinse that leaves hair soft and silky.
- Use a diagonal to separate numbers in a fraction.

    Normally, it takes us 3 1/2 hours to sort the bulk mail at the end of the week.

    You'll need a 1 5/8-inch wrench for this nut.
- Use a diagonal to show line divisions in poetry.

    "Goodnight, goodnight, parting is such sweet sorrow / That I shall say good night 'till it be morrow. / Sleep dwell upon thine eyes and peace in thy breast! / Would I were sleep and peace so sweet to rest!"
- Use a diagonal to indicate *per* or *divided by*.

    The cars in the new fleet average over 25 miles/gallon.

    Shares are calculated in this way: net profit/number of shareholders.

NUMBERS

A few rules guide the use of numbers in writing. In journalistic writing, numbers are preferable to words because they are easier to identify and read. However, a number at the beginning of a sentence is always written as a word. In more formal writing, follow the conventions listed on the next page.

- Use Arabic rather than Roman numerals: *1, 2, 3, 4* rather than *I, II, III, IV.*
- If a number can be written as one or two words, write it as a word. Otherwise, write the numeral: 8, twenty-six, 124, three hundred, 8,549, five million.
- Always write a number at the beginning of sentence as a word even if it is more than two words.

PRACTICE

Add hyphens where they are needed in the following sentences.

1. According to your brain X rays, I see little justification for you to act like a know it all.

2. Father Tan, now an ex priest, reevaluated his theology and became a pro life activist.

3. Syheed's well grounded arguments impressed the crowd of forty five.

4. Ned's time in the four hundred meter freestyle was twenty seven hundredths of a second off the world record time.

5. Following a two hour business venture involving a lemonade stand, the ten year old boy had made a five dollar and fifty cent profit.

Add hyphens, parentheses, brackets, ellipses, and diagonals where they are needed in the following sentences.

6. Muhammad Ali few people remember him as Cassius Clay wrote a poem describing himself as someone who could "… float like a butterflie sic, sting like a bee."

7. Year end bonuses will come in the form of dollars and or vacation days for about three fifths 3 5 of our staff.

8. Before leaving today, please 1 collect the latest sales data 2 add up all the figures and 3 leave them in my left hand drawer.

Skill Building Until Next Time

Look for examples of the punctuation marks from this lesson as you read today. Since they are used less frequently than other marks, you probably won't see them as often. When you do, try to remember how the mark is used. Be especially aware of hyphens, parentheses, brackets, diagonals, and ellipses in advertising copy; check to see if they have been used correctly.

ANSWERS

1. According to your brain X-rays, I see little justification for you to act like a know-it-all.
2. Father Tan, now an ex-priest, re-evaluated his theology and became a pro-life activist.
3. Syheed's well-grounded arguments impressed the crowd of forty-five.
4. Ned's time in the four-hundred-meter freestyle was twenty-seven-hundredths of a second off the world record time.
5. Following a two-hour business venture involving a lemonade stand, the ten-year-old boy had made a five-dollar and fifty-cent profit.
6. Muhammad Ali (few people remember him as Cassius Clay) wrote a poem describing himself as someone who could "... float like a butterflie [sic], sting like a bee."
7. Year-end bonuses will come in the form of dollars and/or vacation days for about three-fifths (3/5) of our staff.
8. Before leaving today, please (1) collect the latest sales data, (2) add up all the figures, and (3) leave them in my left-hand drawer.

L·E·S·S·O·N

VERB TENSE

10

LESSON SUMMARY

Verbs—words for actions or states of being—are what drive written language and give it life. Because verbs are so important, mistakes involving verbs really stand out. This lesson and the next two will help you avoid some of the most common errors with verbs.

Writers use words to establish their credibility. Few things cast doubt on a writer's believability as much as misusing words—especially verbs. Incorrect verb forms call special attention to themselves and bring the writer's education and intelligence into question. Furthermore, once you have mastered the verb forms, you will be able to write clear and persuasive papers and exams.

This lesson explains how to use verbs correctly and highlights a few of the most common mistakes writers make. See how many of the seven errors in verb usage you can find in the **Problem** version of the passage on the following page. In the **Solution** column, the paragraph is rewritten with the correct verb forms. As you go through the lesson, try to apply the rules you learn to these corrections.

Problem

When I was sixteen, my grandmother gave me an heirloom ring that her grandmother had gave her. It was a polished garnet set in hammered silver with two rubies on either side of it. I could of sold it for a small fortune last week. An antique dealer come through town and heard about my ring. He asks to see it. His eyes nearly popped out of his head as he examined it. If I wasn't such a sentimental person, I might have parted with it. But a treasure like that wasn't something you should sell.

Solution

When I was sixteen, my grandmother gave me an heirloom ring that her grandmother had given her. It is a polished garnet set in hammered silver with two rubies on either side of it. I could have sold it for a small fortune last week. An antique dealer came through town and heard about my ring. He asked to see it. His eyes nearly popped out of his head as he examined it. If I weren't such a sentimental person, I might have parted with it. But a treasure like that isn't something you should sell.

PRINCIPAL PARTS OF VERBS

Verbs have three principal parts:

- **Present**—the form of the verb that would complete the sentence, "Today, I _____."
- **Past**—the form of the verb that would complete the sentence, "Yesterday, I _____."
- **Past participle**—the form of the verb that would complete the sentence, "Often, I have _____."

For most verbs, it's easy to form the three pincipal parts if you know the present form. Take the verb *look*, for example. *Today, I look. Yesterday, I looked. Often, I have looked.* For regular verbs, the past and past participle forms both add *-ed* to the present form. But English is full of irregular verbs that form the past and past participle in some other way. The table below shows the principal parts of several often misused verbs.

THREE PRINCIPAL PARTS OF VERBS		
Present	**Past**	**Past Participle***
do	did	done
go	went	gone
see	saw	seen
drink	drank	drunk
break	broke	broken
bring	brought	brought
choose	chose	chosen
know	knew	known
wear	wore	worn
write	wrote	written

* Note: Past participles must be preceeded by the words have, has, *or* had.

PRACTICE

Circle the correct form of the verb in each of the following sentences. The answers can be found at the end of the lesson.

1. The team has certainly (do, did, done) a good job on this presentation.

2. The sales clerk just (throw, threw, thrown) away the opportunity to make a huge commission.

3. The senator (speak, spoke, spoken) at the press conference last Monday.

4. The phone has (ring, rang, rung) only once today.

5. The speaker (come, came) to the point very early in the speech.

6. Harriet (see, saw, seen) the prototype for the new product at the convention.

7. The company has not yet (begin, began, begun) to manufacture its most current model.

8. Has the admitting staff (go, went, gone) to lunch?

9. Heather lost a filling when she (bite, bit, bitten) into the piece of hard candy.

10. Ben couldn't believe that someone had actually (steal, stole, stolen) his car from the ramp.

CONSISTENT VERB TENSE

The tense of a verb tells when an action occurs, occurred, or will occur. Verbs have three basic tenses: present, past, and future. It's important to keep verb tenses consistent as you write. A passage that begins in present tense should continue in present tense. If it begins in past tense, it should stay in past tense. Do not mix tenses.

Wrong:
   Dan **opened** the car door and **looks** for his briefcase.
Correct:
   Dan **opened** the car door and **looked** for his briefcase.
Wrong:
   When we **increase** maintenance services, we **reduced** repair costs.
Correct:
   When we **increase** maintenance services, we **reduce** repair costs.

However, sometimes a writer must show that an action occurred at another time regardless of the tense in which the passage was begun. To allow this, each of these three tenses has three subdivisions: progressive, perfect, and progressive perfect.

PRESENT TENSE FORMS

Present tense shows action that happens now or action that happens routinely. The **present progressive** tense shows an action happening now. An auxiliary verb (*am, is,* or *are*) precedes the *–ing* form (progressive form) of the verb. The **present perfect** tense shows an action that began in the past. An auxiliary verb (*have* or *has*) precedes the past participle form of the verb. The **present perfect progressive** tense also shows action that began in the past and is continuing in the present. Auxiliary verbs (*have been* or *has been*) precede the verb written in its *–ing* form (progressive form).

PRESENT TENSE			
Present	**Progressive**	**Perfect**	**Perfect progressive**
shows action happening now	shows action continuing now	shows action that began in the past, continues now	shows action that began in the past,
Activists *lobby* for change.	Activists *are lobbying* for change.	Activists *have lobbied* for change.	Activists *have been lobbying* for change.
Sulfur *pollutes* the air.	Sulfur *is polluting* the air.	Sulfur *has polluted* the air.	Sulfur *has been polluting* the air.

All the above present tense forms can be used together without constituting a shift in tense. Look at the paragraph below to see how this is done. The verbs are highlighted, and the brackets identify the tense.

I **am writing** [present progressive] to protest the condition of the Mississippi River, from which our city **draws** [present] its drinking water. For years industrial waste **has polluted** [present perfect] its waters, and officials **pay** [present] little attention to the problem. People who live near the river **have been lobbying** [present perfect progressive] for protective legislation, but their efforts **have failed** [present perfect]. I **want** [present] safe water to drink.

PAST TENSE FORMS

Past tense shows action that happened in the past. It uses the past form of the verb. The **past progressive** tense shows a continuing action in the past. An auxiliary verb (*was* or *were*) precedes the progressive (*-ing*) form of the verb. The **past perfect** tense shows an action completed in the past or completed before some other past action.

The auxiliary verb *had* precedes the past participle form of the verb. The **past perfect progressive** tense shows continuing action that began in the past. The auxiliary verbs *had been* precede the progressive form of the verb.

PAST TENSE			
Past	**Progressive**	**Perfect**	**Perfect progressive**
occurred in the past	continuing action in the past	completed prior to another action	continuing action started in the past
Local officials *spoke* to the management.	Local officials *were speaking* to the management.	Local officials *had spoken* to the management.	Local officials *had been speaking* to the management.
The reporter *covered* the meetings.	The reporter *was covering* the meetings.	The reporter *had covered* the meetings.	The reporter *had been covering* the meetings.

All of the above past tense forms can be used together in writing a passage without constituting a shift in tense. The paragraph below illustrates how this is done. The verbs are highlighted for you, and the brackets identify the tense.

Last year, local officials **cited** [past] a manufacturing company in our county for improperly disposing of hazardous waste. The company **ignored** [past] the action and **continued** [past] to dump its waste as they **had been doing**.[past perfect progressive] They **had dumped** [past perfect] waste the same way for years and **planned** [past] to continue. Several months later the residue **seeped** [past] into the drinking water supply. A local environmentalist, who **had been tracking** [past perfect progressive] the company's dumping procedures, alerted local officials. They fined the company $3,000 for damages, but the company **has** never **paid** [past perfect] the fine.

FUTURE TENSE FORMS

Future tense shows action that has yet to happen. The auxiliary verbs *will, would,* or *shall* precede the present form of the verb. The **future progressive** tense shows continuing actions in the future. The auxiliary verb phrases *will be, shall be,* or *would be* precede the progressive form of the verb. The **future perfect** tense shows actions that will be completed at a certain time in the future. The auxiliary verb phrases *will have, would have,* or *will have been* precede the past participle form of the verb. The **future perfect progressive** tense shows continuing actions that will be completed at a certain time in the future. The verb phrases *will have been, would have been,* or *shall have been* precede the progressive form of the verb.

FUTURE TENSE			
Future	**Progressive**	**Perfect**	**Perfect progressive**
action that will happen	continuing action that will happen	action that will be completed by a certain time	continuing action that will be completed by a certain time
We *will begin* a letter-writing campaign.	Everyone *will be writing* letters.	By summer, we *will have written* reams of letters.	Legislators *will have been receiving* letters throughout the year.
Newspapers *will cover* this case.	Newspapers *will be covering* this case.	By summer, every newspaper *will have written* about this case.	Newspapers *will have been covering* the case throughout the year.

All of the above future tense forms can be used together in writing a paragraph. They do not constitute a shift in tense. The paragraph below illustrates how this is done. The verbs are highlighted for you, and the brackets identify the tense.

Starting next week, we **will reduce** [future] the money we spend on waste disposal. We **will do** [future] this because our public relations costs have skyrocketed during the year. Since no one in the community **will sell** [future] land to us to use for waste disposal, we **will be relocating** [future progressive] in a new community with a better business environment. This move **would put** [future] over three hundred employees out of work. It **would reduce** [future] the amount of consumer dollars spent at local businesses.

By this time next year, nearly one thousand people **will have lost** [future perfect] their jobs. Your business leaders **will have been looking** [future perfect progressive] for ways to replace lost revenue. Furthermore, legislators **will be meddling** [future progressive] in our local affairs, and the news media **will have portrayed** [future perfect] us all as fools.

HOW VERB TENSES CONVEY MEANING

Managing verb tense carefully helps writers avoid the confusion that comes with thoughtless use. The examples below illustrate how verb tense can completely change the meaning of a sentence.

Example:

Beth discovered that Nick had left work and gone home.

Beth discovered that Nick had left work and went home.

In the first sentence, because *gone* is the participle form, it goes with *had left* in the second part of the sentence. So Nick is the one who *had gone* home. In the second sentence, *went* is in the simple past tense like *discovered* in the first part of the sentence. So this time it's Beth who *went* home.

Example:

Cory told the officer that she had answered the phone and drank a can of soda pop.

Cory told the officer that she had answered the phone and had drunk a can of soda pop.

In the first sentence, *drank* is in the same tense as *told*—they're both past tense. So Cory was drinking around the same time as she was telling. In the second sentence, *had drunk* matches *had answered,* so in this case Cory was drinking around the time she answered the phone.

HAVE, NOT *OF*

When forming the various perfect tenses, people sometimes write *of* when they should write *have*, probably because they are writing what they hear. *I should've* (*should've* is a contraction of *should have*) sounds a lot like *I should of.* But the proper form in writing is *have*, not *of.*

Wrong:

I **could of** seen the difference if I had looked more closely.

Correct:

I **could have** seen the difference if I had looked more closely.

Wrong:

The park ranger **should of** warned the campers about the bears.

Correct:

The park ranger **should have** warned the campers about the bears.

SWITCHING VERB TENSES

Sometimes you have to switch from past tense to present to avoid implying an untruth.

Wrong:

I met the new technician. He **was** very personable. [What happened? Did he die?]

Correct:

I met the new technician. He **is** very personable.

Wrong:

We went to the new Italian restaurant on Vine last night. The atmosphere **was** wonderful. [What happened? Did it burn down during the night?]

Correct:

We went to the new Italian restaurant on Vine last night. The atmosphere **is** wonderful.

Even if a passage is written in past tense, a statement that continues to be true is written in present tense.

Examples:

During Galileo's time few people **believed** [past] that the earth **revolves** [present] around the sun.

The building engineer **explained** [past] to the plumber that the pipes **run** [present] parallel to the longest hallway in the building.

SUBJUNCTIVE MOOD

When Tevya in *Fiddler on the Roof* sings, "If I were a rich man. . .," he uses the verb *were* to signal that he is, in fact, not a rich man. Normally, the verb *was* would be used with the subject *I*, but *were* serves a special purpose. This is called the subjunctive *were*. It indicates a condition that is contrary to fact.

Examples:

If I **were** a cat, I could sleep all day long and never have to worry about work.

If he **were** more attentive to details, he could be a copyeditor.

PRACTICE

Circle the correct verb form in each of the following sentences.

11. Before I opened the door, I (ring, rang, had rung) the doorbell.

12. By the time I get to Phoenix, he will (read, have read) my goodbye letter.

13. The scientist explained why Saturn (is, was) surrounded by rings.

14. I would ask for a transfer if I (was, were) you.

15. The leaves on the trees have already (begin, began, begun) to fall.

16. The doctor took my pulse and (measures, measured) my blood pressure.

17. The president wishes he would (of, have) taken a stock option rather than a salary increase.

18. Boswick wishes he would have ordered a bigger sweatshirt because his (is, was) too small.

19. Ms. Grey announced that the floor manager (is, was) responsible for work schedules.

20. We could cut transportation costs if the plant (was, were) closer to the retail outlets.

Skill Building Until Next Time

Listen carefully to people today. Do you hear common errors such as "I *could of* gone out if I had done my work"? Once you make it a habit to listen for verb choice errors, you'll realize how many people make them. Some mistakes are so accepted that they might not sound strange at first. The more sensitive you are to grammatical errors, the less likely you'll be to make them yourself—in both writing and speaking.

ANSWERS

1. done	6. saw	11. had rung	16. measured
2. threw	7. begun	12. have read	17. have
3. spoke	8. gone	13. is	18. is
4. rung	9. bit	14. were	19. is
5. came	10. stolen	15. begun	20. were

USING VERBS TO CREATE STRONG WRITING

11

LESSON SUMMARY

If verbs drive meaning, lively verbs really make your writing accelerate. This lesson shows you how to use verbs to capture readers' interest.

F
ew people bother to read uninteresting writing. Even if they read it, they may not absorb the message. This lesson discusses ways to use verbs that will make your writing lively and interesting for the reader. Read the two paragraphs on the next page. Which one seems livelier, more interesting? The paragraphs tell an identical story, but one of them uses verbs effectively to tell the story in such a way that it is more likely to be remembered. The sentences are presented one at a time, side by side so you can make the comparison more easily.

Problem	Solution
When my brother was asked by the local Rotary Club to speak to them about computer programming, our entire family was amazed by the request.	When the local Rotary Club asked my brother to speak to them about computer programming, the request amazed our entire family.
A gasp was made by mother, a laugh was emitted by my father, and my head was shaken by me.	My mother gasped, my father laughed, and I just shook my head.
My brother is considered by us to be a shy, quiet computer nerd.	We consider my brother a shy, quiet computer nerd.
Since I am regarded by my family as the creative one, I was assigned by my brother the task of creating the visual aids.	Since everyone in the family regards me as the creative one, my brother assigned me the task of creating the visual aids.
The information was organized by my father.	My father organized the information.
Formal invitations were requested by my mother from the Rotary Club secretary and were sent by her to all of our friends.	My mother requested formal invitations from the Rotary Club secretary and sent them to all of our friends.
Organizing and rehearsing of the presentation was worked on by my family until 10:00 P.M. the night before the presentation.	Our family worked until 10:00 P.M. the night before the presentation, organizing and rehearsing.
The fact that he was ready was known by us.	We knew he was ready.
That night three feet of snow was dumped by the skies. The city was paralyzed, and all work and activities were canceled, including the Rotary Club meeting and my brother's presentation.	That night the skies dumped three feet of snow, paralyzing the city and causing all work and activities to be canceled, including the Rotary Club meeting and my brother's presentation.

ACTIVE VS. PASSIVE VOICE

When the subject of a sentence performs the action of the verb, we say the sentence is active. Write using active verbs to make your writing more conversational and interesting. In a sentence with an active verb, the person or thing that performs the action is named before the verb, or the action word(s), in a sentence. This may sound confusing, but the following examples illustrate the difference. The italicized words show who is performing the action. The underlined words are verbs.

Passive Verbs	Active Verbs
I <u>was taken</u> to my first horse show by my *grandfather*.	My *grandfather* <u>took</u> me to my first horse show.
I <u>was taught</u> to fish by my *mother* almost before I <u>was taught</u> to walk.	My *mother* <u>taught</u> me to fish almost before *I* <u>learned</u> to walk.

In each of the active verb sentences, the person performing the action is named first. If you look more closely at these examples, you'll notice that the active verb versions are shorter and clearer. They sound more like natural conversation. Strive for these qualities in your writing. The following table illustrates the difference between active and passive voice in several of the verb tenses you learned about in Lesson 10.

Verb Tense	Active Voice	Passive Voice
Present	The *clerk* <u>opens</u> the mail.	The mail <u>is opened</u> by the *clerk*.
Past	The *clerk* <u>opened</u> the mail.	The mail <u>was opened</u> by the *clerk*.
Future	The *clerk* <u>will open</u> the mail.	The mail <u>will be opened</u> by the *clerk*.
Present Perfect	The *clerk* <u>has opened</u> the mail.	The mail <u>has been opened</u> by the *clerk*.
Past Perfect	The *clerk* <u>had opened</u> the mail.	The mail <u>had been opened</u> by the *clerk*.
Future Perfect	The *clerk* <u>will have opened</u> the mail.	The mail <u>will have been opened</u> by the *clerk*.

Most writers prefer active voice to passive voice because it makes the writing active, more alive. Generally, readers find active writing easier to read and remember. In both of the tables above, you can see that active voice sentences tend to be shorter than passive ones.

PRACTICE

Choose the sentence that is written in active voice from each of the following sets. The answers to each set of questions can be found at the end of the lesson.

1. a. Janice carefully packed the china.
   b. The china was carefully packed by Janice.

2. a. The CDs were purchased by my mother.
   b. My mother purchased the CDs.

3. a. Forty black candles were put on my mother's cake by Dad.
   b. Dad put forty black candles on my mother's cake.

4. a. The snow will be cleared by the plow.
   b. The plow will clear the snow.

5. a. Citizens believe that judges do not hand out adequate penalties for drug dealers.
   b. It is believed by the citizens that adequate penalties for drug dealers are not being handed out by judges.

6. a. Coins are often thrown in fountains by tourists.
   b. Tourists often throw coins in fountains.

7. a. Every Sunday morning millions of children watch TV.
   b. Every Sunday morning TV is being watched by millions of children.

WHEN TO USE PASSIVE VOICE

In addition to lacking life, the passive voice can also signal an unwillingness to take responsibility for actions or an intention to discourage questioning. The following sentence illustrates this.

It has been recommended that twenty workers be laid off within the next three months.

The passive voice here is intended to make a definite statement of fact, one that will not be questioned. It leaves no loose ends. Dictators often write and speak in passive voice. A thoughtful person will see past the passive voice and ask questions anyway. Who is recommending this action? Why? Who will be doing the laying off? How will workers be chosen?

Passive voice is not always bad, however. Sometimes, though rarely, it actually works better than active voice. The situations when passive voice is preferable to active voice are outlined below.

1. When the object is more important than the agent of action (the doer).

Sometimes in scientific writing the object is the focus rather than the doer. The following paragraph is written in both passive and active voice, respectively. The first paragraph is more appropriate in this case because the operation, not the doctor, is the focus of the action. The passage cannot be written in active voice without placing the emphasis on the doer, the doctor. Therefore, passive voice is the better choice in this instance.

Passive voice

The three-inch incision is made right above the pubic bone. Plastic clips are used to clamp off blood vessels and minimize bleeding. The skin is folded back and secured with clamps. Next, the stomach muscle is cut at a fifteen-degree angle, right top to bottom left.

Active voice

The doctor makes a three-inch incision right above the pubic bone. He uses plastic clips to clamp off the blood vessels and minimize bleeding. He folds back the skin and secures it with clamps. Next, he cuts the stomach muscle at a fifteen-degree angle, right top to bottom left.

2. When the agent of action (doer) is unknown or secret.

Sometimes a newswriter will protect a source by writing, "It was reported that…." In other instances, perhaps no one knows who perpetrated an action: "First State Bank was robbed…."

3. When passive voice results in shorter sentences without detracting from the meaning.

Generally, active voice is shorter and more concise than passive voice. However, there are a few exceptions. Examine the examples in the table below. If using passive voice saves time and trouble, in addition to resulting in a shorter sentence, use it.

Active	Passive
The designers of the study told the interviewer to give interviewees an electric shock each time they smiled.	The interviewer was told to give the interviewees an electric shock each time they smiled.
The police apprehended Axtell, the detectives interrogated him, and the grand jury indicted him.	Axtell was apprehended, interrogated, and indicted.

OTHER LIFE-DRAINING VERB CONSTRUCTIONS

If thought is a train, then verbs are the wheels that carry the cargo along. The thought will move more quickly if it is transported by many big, strong wheels. Here are some constructions to avoid and how to choose bigger, better verbs instead.

USING STATE-OF-BEING VERBS

State-of-being verbs are all the forms of *be: am, is, are, was, were,* and so on. State-of-being verbs don't do as much as action verbs to move meaning. In our train-of-thought analogy, state-of-being verbs are very tiny wheels, incapable of moving big thoughts quickly or easily. If you have only trivial things to say, by all means, use state-of-being verbs. If your ideas are more complex or interesting, they will require bigger and better verbs.

Look at the paragraph on the next page. In the first version, most of the verbs are state-of-being verbs. In the second version, action verbs make the paragraph more interesting.

State-of-being verbs

The class was outside during noon recess. The sunshine was bright. Earlier in the day there was rain, but later the weather was pleasant. The breeze was slight; the newly fallen leaves were in motion. Across the street from the school was an ice cream truck. It was what the children were looking at longingly.

Action verbs

The class played outside during noon recess. The sun shone brightly. Earlier in the day, rain had fallen, but later pleasant weather arrived. A slight breeze blew the newly fallen leaves. The children looked longingly at the ice cream truck across the street.

TURNING VERBS INTO NOUNS

Naturally, if you take the wheels off the train of thought and put them on a flatbed as cargo, the train will not move as well. Look at the two sentences below. In the first one, several verbs have been turned into nouns in order to make the writing sound "intellectual." This "verbification" actually makes the writing more difficult to read. The second sentence communicates the same information with the same amount of sophistication, but turning the nouns back into verbs makes it easier to read. Verb forms are highlighted to make them easier to identify.

The customer service division **is** now **conducting** an assessment of its system for the reaction to consumer concerns and the development of new products.

The customer service division **is assessing** its system for **reacting** to consumer concerns and **developing** new products.

ADDING UNNECESSARY AUXILIARY VERBS

Generally, if you don't need an auxiliary verb (*have, had, is, are, was, were, will, would*, and so on) to carry meaning (see Lesson 10), don't use one.

Unnessary Auxiliary Verbs	Corrected Version
After lunch we *would meet* in the lounge.	After lunch we *met* in the lounge.
The temperature *was rising* steadily.	The temperature *rose* steadily.
Every morning the doors *will open* at 8:00.	Every morning the doors *open* at 8:00.

STARTING WITH *THERE* OR *IT*

Many sentences unnecessarily begin with *there is/are/was/were* or with *it is/was*. Usually all those words do is postpone the beginning of the actual thought. The sentences on the next page illustrate how these life-draining words can be removed from your writing.

Unnecessary *There* or *It*	Corrected Version
There are three people who are authorized to use this machinery.	Three people are authorized to use this machinery.
There is one good way to handle this problem: to ignore it.	One good way to handle this problem is to ignore it.
It was a perfect evening for a rocket launch.	The evening was perfect for a rocket launch.
There were several people standing in line waiting for the bus.	Several people stood in line waiting for the bus.

USE LIVELY, INTERESTING VERBS

If you want to move thought efficiently, work for precision and look for verbs that create an image in the reader's mind. Compare the sentences below to see this principle in action.

Dull	Lively
At my barbershop, someone does your nails and your shoes while your hair is being cut.	At my barbershop, someone manicures your nails and shines your shoes as your hair is cut.
Violent cartoons are harmful to children's emotional development and sense of reality.	Violent cartoons stunt children's emotional development and distort their sense of reality.

PRACTICE

Choose the best sentence from each set below. Keep in mind what you have learned about verbs in this lesson.

8. a. Much concern is being voiced by the citizens over the failure to balance the budget.
   b. Citizens are voicing much concern over the failure to balance the budget.

9. a. The game was played by three old men and a young boy.
   b. Three old men and a young boy played the game.

10. a. Those who evaluate law enforcement officers consider procedures that avoid lawsuits more valuable than those that effectively enforce the laws.
   b. Those responsible for the evaluation of law enforcement officers have a greater consideration for the discharge of procedures that will result in the avoidance of lawsuits than those resulting in effective enforcement of the laws.

11. a. There are many reasons that you should avoid foods that are high in fat.

b. You should avoid high fat foods for many reasons.

12. a. After dinner every night we would make popcorn.

b. We made popcorn every night after dinner.

13. a. We gobbled up donuts every morning before work.

b. We had donuts every morning before work.

14. a. A computer technician must have solid people skills.

b. It is necessary for a computer technician to have solid people skills.

Skill Building Until Next Time

As you read newspapers, magazines, textbooks, or other materials today, look for examples of sentences in active voice and in passive voice. Try converting some passive voice sentences into active voice and vice versa. Which version is more effective?

ANSWERS

1. a.	**5.** a.	**9.** b.	**13.** a.
2. b.	**6.** b.	**10.** a.	**14.** a.
3. b.	**7.** a.	**11.** b.	
4. b.	**8.** b.	**12.** b.	

SUBJECT-VERB AGREEMENT

LESSON SUMMARY

Without thinking about it, you usually make sure your subjects and verbs agree, both in speaking and in writing. Only a few situations cause difficulty in subject-verb agreement. This lesson will show you how to deal with those few situations in your writing.

When a subject in a clause—the person or thing doing the action—matches the verb in number, we say the subject and verb *agree*. Most native English speakers have little trouble matching subjects with the correct verbs. A few grammatical constructions pose most of the problems. This lesson explains the concept of subject-verb agreement and provides practice in those problem areas.

AGREEMENT BETWEEN NOUN SUBJECTS AND VERBS

In written language, a subject must agree with its verb in number. In other words, if a subject is singular, the verb must be singular. If the subject is plural, the verb must be plural. If you are unsure whether a verb is singular or plural, apply this simple test. Fill in the blanks in the two sentences below with the matching form of the verb. The verb form that best completes the first sentence is singular. The verb form that best completes the second sentence is plural.

Singular   **Plural**
One person _____.   Two people _____.

Look at these examples using the verbs *speak, do,* and *was.* Try it yourself with any verb that confuses you. Unlike nouns, verbs ending in *s* are usually singular.

Singular	Plural
One person <u>speaks</u>.	**Two people <u>speak</u>.**
One person <u>does</u>.	Two people <u>do</u>.
One person <u>was</u>.	Two people <u>were</u>.

SPECIAL PROBLEMS

Doesn't/Don't and Wasn't/Weren't

Some people have particular trouble with *doesn't/don't* (contractions for *does not* and *do not*) and with *wasn't/weren't* (contractions for *was not* and *were not*). *Doesn't* and *wasn't* are singular; *don't* and *weren't* are plural. If you say the whole phrase instead of the contraction, you'll usually get the right form.

Phrases Following the Subject

Pay careful attention to the subject in a sentence. Do not allow a phrase following it to mislead you into using a verb that does not agree with the subject. The subjects and verbs are highlighted in the following examples.

One of the print orders **is** missing.
The software **designs** by Liu Chen **are** complex and colorful.
A **handbook** with thorough instructions **comes** with this product.
The **president**, along with her three executive assistants, **leaves** for the conference tomorrow.

Special Singular Subjects

Some nouns are singular even though they end in *s*. Despite the plural form, they require a singular verb because we think of them as a single thing. Most of the nouns in the following list are singular. Some can be either singular or plural, depending on their use in the sentence.

measles	physics	sports
mumps	economics	politics
news	mathematics	statistics
checkers	civics	
marbles (the game)	athletics	

Here are some examples of how these words work in sentences.

The **news is** on at 6:00.

Checkers is my favorite game.

Sports is a healthy way to reduce stress.

Low-impact **sports are** recommended for older adults.

Words stating a single amount or a time require a singular verb. Examine a sentence carefully to see if the amount or time is considered a single measure.

Two dollars **is** the price of that small replacement part. [single amount]

Two dollars **are** lying on my dresser.

Three hours **was** required to complete this simulation. [single measure]

Three hours of each day **were** spent rehearsing.

Three-quarters of her time **is** spent writing.

PRACTICE

Circle the correct verb in each of the following sentences. The answers to each set of questions can be found at the end of the lesson.

1. When the comedian (jokes, joke), the audience members (laughs, laugh).

2. A single flower now (grows, grow) where the trees used to (grows, grow).

3. Manuel (speaks, speak) English, but his parents (speaks, speak) Spanish.

4. The clerk (rings, ring) up the sales while the customers (waits, wait) in line.

5. The sopranos (hums, hum) softly while the tenor soloist (sings, sing)

6. The new colors (doesn't, don't) look especially appealing.

7. The door to the building (wasn't, weren't) locked last night.

8. The drive-up teller line (doesn't, don't) open until 9:30 on Saturday mornings.

9. Marge didn't receive the message because the phones (wasn't, weren't) working.

10. He (doesn't, don't) remember if the ties (is, are) still on sale.

11. One of the clerks (is, are) sorting the rack of trousers that (was, were) mislabeled.

12. The petty cash box, along with the ticket receipts, (is, are) turned in at the end of the day.

13. These statistics (is, are) the result of a flawed study.

14. Statistics (was, were) my most difficult math course in high school.

15. Half of the bagel (was, were) eaten.

16. Half of the bagels (was, were) eaten.

AGREEMENT BETWEEN PRONOUN SUBJECTS AND VERBS

Pronoun subjects present a problem for even the most sophisticated speakers of English. Some pronouns are always singular; others are always plural. A handful of pronouns can be either singular or plural.

SINGULAR PRONOUNS

These pronouns are always singular.

each	anybody	everyone	one
either	anyone	no one	somebody
neither	everybody	nobody	someone

The pronouns in the first column are the ones most likely to be misused. You can avoid a mismatch by mentally adding the word *one* after the pronoun and removing the other words between the pronoun and the verb. Look at the following examples to see how this is done.

> Each of the men wants his own car.
> Each *one* wants his own car.
> Either of the salesclerks knows where the sale merchandise is located.
> Either *one* knows where the sale merchandise is located.

These sentences may sound awkward because so many speakers misuse these pronouns, and you have probably become accustomed to hearing them used incorrectly. Despite that, the substitution trick (*one* for the words following the pronoun) will help you avoid this mistake.

WATCH OUT FOR QUESTIONS

With questions beginning with *has* or *have*, remember that *has* is singular while *have* is plural. Pay special attention to the verb-subject combination in a question. In fact, the correct verb is easier to identify if you turn the question into a statement.

Question Form	Statement Form
(Is, Are) some of the customers noticing the difference?	Some of the customers **are** noticing the difference.
(Has, Have) either of the shipments arrived?	Either [*one*] of the shipments **has** arrived.
(Does, Do) each of the terminals have a printer?	Each [*one*] of the terminals **does** have a printer.

PLURAL PRONOUNS

These pronouns are always plural and require a plural verb.

both	many
few	several

SINGULAR/PLURAL PRONOUNS

The following pronouns can be either singular or plural. The words or prepositional phrases following them determine whether they are singular or plural. If the phrase following the pronoun contain a plural noun or pronoun, the verb must be plural. If the phrase following the pronoun contains a singular noun or pronoun, the verb must be singular. See how this is done in the sentences following the list of pronouns. The key words are highlighted.

all	none
any	some
most	

Singular	Plural
All of the **work is** finished.	**All** of the **jobs are** finished.
Is any of the **pizza** left?	**Are** any of the **pieces** of pizza left?
Most of the **grass has** turned brown.	**Most** of the **blades** of grass **have** turned brown.
None of the **time was** wasted.	**None** of the **minutes were** wasted.
Some of the **fruit was** spoiled.	**Some** of the **apples were** spoiled.

PRACTICE

Circle the correct verb in each of the following sentences. Answers are at the end of the lesson.

17. Neither of these keys (unlocks, unlock) the back door.

18. Each of the community profiles (takes, take) a creative approach to advertising.

19. All of the tasks (has, have) been assigned.

20. Some of the residents (was, were) pleased with the new development.

21. Either of these light fixtures (is, are) suitable for my office.

22. (Was, Were) any of the samples defective?

23. (Do, Does) each of the phones have multiple lines?

24. (Has, Have) either of the partners announced an intention to reorganize?

25. Neither of our largest accounts (needs, need) to be serviced at this time.

26. Both of the applicants (seems, seem) qualified.

27. A woman in one of my classes (works, work) at the Civic Center box office.

28. None of our resources (goes, go) to outside consultants.

29. A good knowledge of the rules (helps, help) you understand the game.

30. Each of these prescriptions (causes, cause) bloating and irritability.

31. (Have, Has) either of them ever arrived on time?

SPECIAL SENTENCE STRUCTURES

COMPOUND SUBJECTS

■ If two nouns or pronouns are joined by *and*, they require a plural verb.

He and she **want** to buy a new house.

Jack and Jill **want** to buy a new house.

■ If two singular nouns or pronouns are joined by *or* or *nor*, they require a singular verb. Think of them as two separate sentences and you'll never make a mistake in agreement.

Jack or Jill **wants** to buy a new house.

Jack **wants** to buy a new house.

Jill **wants** to buy a new house.

■ Singular and plural subjects joined by *or* or *nor* require a verb that agrees with the subject closest to the verb.

Neither management nor the **employees like** the new agreement.

Neither the employees nor the **management likes** the new agreement.

MAKE SURE YOU FIND THE SUBJECT

Verbs agree with the subject, not the complement, of a sentence. The verb, a form of *be*, links the subject and the complement, but usually the subject comes first and the complement comes after the verb.

Taxes were the main challenge facing the financial department.

The main **challenge** facing the financial department **was** taxes.

A serious **problem** for most automobile commuters **is** traffic jams.

Traffic jams are a serious problem for most automobile commuters.

Questions and Sentences Beginning with *There* or *Here*

When a sentence asks a question or begins with the words *there* or *here*, the subject follows the verb. Locate the subject of the sentence and make certain the verb matches it. In the examples below, the subjects and verbs are highlighted in the corrected forms.

Wrong	Corrected
What is the conditions of the contract?	What **are** the **conditions** of the contract?
Why is her reports always so disorganized?	Why **are** her **reports** always so disorganized?
Here's the records you requested.	Here **are** the **records** you requested.
There is four people seeking this promotion.	There **are** four **people** seeking this promotion.

Inverted Sentences

Inverted sentences also contain subjects that follow, rather than precede, the verbs. Locate the subject in the sentence and make certain the verb agrees with it. In the example sentences below, the subjects and verbs in the corrected sentences are highlighted.

Wrong	Correct
Beside the front desk stands three new vending machines.	Beside the front desk **stand** three new vending **machines**.
Suddenly, out of the thicket comes three large bucks.	Suddenly, out of the thicket **come** three large **bucks**.
Along with our highest recommendation goes our best wishes in your new job.	Along with our highest recommendation **go** our best **wishes** in your new job.

PRACTICE

Circle the correct verb in each of the following sentences. Answers are at the end of the lesson.

32. Every other day either Bert or Ernie (takes, take) out the trash.

33. Neither the style nor the color (matches, match) what we currently have.

34. Either the associates or the manager (orders, order) the merchandise.

35. Either the manager or the associates (orders, order) the merchandise.

36. (Is, Are) the men's wear or the women's wear department on the ground floor?

37. Mr. Jefson's passion (is, are) economics.

38. (Was, Were) there any furniture sets left over after the sale?

39. There (isn't, aren't) many days left before the Grand Opening.

40. Here (is, are) the information you requested.

41. Off into the horizon (runs, run) the herd of buffalo.

Skill Building Until Next Time

Listen to people as they speak. Do they use verbs correctly? Do they use the correct tense? Do the subjects and verb match? It's probably not a good idea to correct your family, friends, and fellow students, but you can give yourself some good practice by listening for mistakes.

ANSWERS

1. jokes, laugh
2. grows, grow
3. speaks, speak
4. rings, wait
5. hum, sings
6. don't
7. wasn't
8. doesn't
9. weren't
10. doesn't, are
11. is, was
12. is
13. are
14. was
15. was
16. were
17. unlocks
18. takes
19. have
20. were
21. is

22. Were
23. Does
24. Has
25. needs
26. seem
27. works
28. go
29. helps
30. causes
31. Has
32. takes
33. matches
34. orders
35. order
36. Is
37. is
38. Were
39. aren't
40. is
41. runs

L·E·S·S·O·N
USING PRONOUNS

13

LESSON SUMMARY

Pronouns are so often *misused* in speech that many people don't really know how to avoid pronoun errors in writing. This lesson shows you how to avoid the most common pronoun errors.

A pronoun is a word that is used in place of a noun. Pronouns that are misused call attention to themselves and detract from the message of a piece of writing. This lesson explains the basic principles of pronoun use and highlights the most common pronoun problems: agreement, case, noun-pronoun pairs, incomplete constructions, ambiguous pronoun references, and reflexive pronouns.

PRONOUNS AND ANTECEDENTS

The noun represented by a pronoun is called its *antecedent*. The prefix *ante* means *to come before*. Usually, the antecedent comes before the pronoun in a sentence. In the following example sentences, the pronouns are italicized and the antecedents (the words they represent) are underlined.

The government <u>workers</u> received *their* paychecks.
<u>Jane</u> thought *she* saw the missing <u>boy</u> and reported *him* to the police.
The shift <u>supervisor</u> hates these <u>accidents</u> because *he* thinks *they* can be easily avoided.

A pronoun must match the number of its antecedent. In other words, if the antecedent is singular, the pronoun must be singular. If the antecedent is plural, the pronoun must be plural. Few people make mistakes when matching a pronoun with a noun antecedent. However, sometimes a pronoun is the antecedent for a another pronoun. Indefinite pronoun antecedents frequently result in a number mismatch between pronoun and antecedent. In Lesson 12 you learned about singular pronouns. Here is the list again.

each	anybody	everyone	one
either	anyone	no one	somebody
neither	everybody	nobody	someone

- A pronoun with one of the words from this list as its antecedent must be singular.

  <u>Each</u> (singular) of the men brought *his* (singular) favorite tool to the bachelor party.

  <u>Everyone</u> (singular) who wants to be in the "Toughman" contest should pay up *his* (singular) life insurance.

  <u>Somebody</u> left *her* purse underneath the desk.

  <u>Neither</u> of the occupants could locate *his* (or *her*) key to the apartment.

- If two or more singular nouns or pronouns are joined by *and*, use a plural pronoun.

  <u>Buddha and Muhammad</u> built religions around *their* philosophies.

  If <u>he and she</u> want to know where I was, *they* should ask me.

- If two or more singular nouns or pronouns are joined by *or*, use a singular pronoun.

  Matthew or Jacob will loan you *his* calculator.

  The <u>elephant or the moose</u> will furiously protect *its* young.

- If a singular and a plural noun or pronoun are joined by *or*, the pronoun agrees with the closest noun or pronoun it represents.

  Neither the soldiers nor the <u>sergeant</u> was sure of *his* location.

  Neither the sergeant nor the <u>soldiers</u> were sure of *their* location.

PRACTICE

Circle the correct pronoun in each of the following sentences. The answers to each set of questions can be found at the end of the lesson.

1. No one in (her, their) right mind would agree to drive that contraption.

2. Neither the students nor the teacher brought (his, their) book to class.

3. Anyone who wants a ticket to the banquet should sign (his, their) name on this sheet.

4. Ask someone in this office where the instruction manual is, and (he, they) probably can't tell you.

5. Neither Alexis nor Heidi will inconvenience (herself, themselves) to cover your mistake.

6. If you break a print head or a roller on the printer, (it, they) is hard to replace.

7. I know of someone who might give you (her, their) notes from the course.

8. Almost anybody can improve (his, their) writing by using this book.

9. If you want to make a good impression on a customer, don't talk down to (her, them).

PRONOUN CASE

Most people have no trouble knowing when to use *I*, when to use *me*, or when to use *my*. These three pronouns illustrate the three cases of the first person singular pronoun: nominative (*I*), objective (*me*), and possessive (*my*). The table below shows the cases of all the personal pronouns, both singular and plural.

PERSONAL PRONOUN CASE		
Nominative	**Objective**	**Possessive**
I	me	my
we	us	our
you	you	your
he	him	his
she	her	her
they	them	their
it	it	its

Nominative case pronouns (those in the first column) are used as subjects or as complements following linking verbs (*am, is, are, was, were*—any form of *be*). Nominative case pronouns following a linking verb may sound strange to you because so few people use them correctly.

> **They** left a few minutes early in order to mail the package. [subject]
> **I** looked all over town for the type of paper you wanted. [subject]
> The doctor who removed my appendix was **he**. [follows a linking verb]
> "This is **she**, or it is **I**," said Barbara into the phone. [follows a linking verb]
> The winners of the sales contest were **he** and **she**. [follows a linking verb]

Objective case pronouns (those in the middle column in the table) are used as objects following an action verb or as objects of a preposition.

> The help line representative gave **him** an answer over the phone. [follows an action verb]
> Of all these samples, I prefer **them**. [follows an action verb]
> We went to lunch with Sammy and **him**. [object of the preposition *with*]
> We couldn't tell whether the package was for **them** or **us**. [object(s) of the preposition *for*]

Possessive case pronouns (those in the third column in the table) show ownership. Few English speakers misuse the possessive case pronouns. Most pronoun problems occur with the nominative and objective cases.

PROBLEMS WITH PRONOUN CASE

A single pronoun in a sentence is easy to use correctly. In fact, most English speakers would readily identify the mistakes in the following sentences.

> **Me** worked on the project with **he**.
> My neighbor gave **she** a ride to work.

Most people know that **Me** in the first sentence should be **I** and that **he** should be **him**. They would also know that **she** in the second sentence should be **her**. Such errors are easy to spot when the pronouns are used alone in a sentence. The problem occurs when a pronoun is used with a noun or another pronoun. See if you can spot the errors in the following sentences.

> **Wrong:**
> The grand marshall rode with Shane and I.
> Donna and me are going to the Civic Center.
> The stage manager spoke to my brother and I.

The errors in these sentences are harder to see than those in the sentences with a single pronoun. If you turn the sentence with two pronouns into two separate sentences, the error becomes very obvious.

> **Correct:**
> The grand marshall rode with Shane.
> The grand marshall rode with **me** (not *I*).
> Donna is going to the Civic Center. [Use the singular verb *is* in place of *are*.]
> **I** (not *me*) am going to the Civic Center. [Use the verb *am* in place of *are*.]
> The stage manager spoke to my brother.
> The stage manager spoke to **me** (not *I*).

Splitting a sentence in two does not work as well with the preposition *between*. If you substitute *with* for *between*, then the error is easier to spot.

The problem is between (she, her) and (I, me).

The problem is with **her**. (not *she*)

The problem is with **me**. (not *I*)

PRACTICE

Circle the correct pronouns in the following sentences. Answers are at the end of the lesson.

10. Andy or Arvin will bring (his, their) camera so (he, they) can take pictures of the party.

11. Benny and (he, him) went to the movies with Bonnie and (I, me).

12. Neither my cousins nor my uncle knows what (he, they) will do tomorrow.

13. Why must it always be (I, me) who cleans up the lounge?

14. The pilot let (he, him) and (I, me) look at the instrument panel.

15. Have you heard the latest news about (she, her) and (they, them)?

16. My friend and (I, me) both want to move to another location.

NOUN-PRONOUN PAIRS

Sometimes a noun is immediately followed by a pronoun in a sentence. To make certain you use the correct pronoun, delete the noun from the pair. Look at the following examples to see how this is done.

PRONOUNS IN NOUN-PRONOUN PAIRS

Which Pronoun?	Remove the Noun
(We, Us) support personnel wish to lodge a complaint.	**We** wish to lodge a complaint.
They gave the job to (we, us) inventory staffers.	They gave the job to **us**.
The committee threw (we, us) retirees a huge end-of-the-year party.	The committee threw **us** a huge end-of-the-year party.

INCOMPLETE CONSTRUCTIONS

Sometimes a pronoun comes at the end of a sentence following a comparative word such as *than* or *as*.

> Harold spent as much time on this project as (they, them).
> Duane can build cabinets better than (I, me).
> The long day exhausted us more than (they, them).
> My youngest child is now taller than (I, me).

In each of these sentences part of the meaning is implied. To figure out which pronoun is correct, complete the sentence in your head and use the pronoun that makes more sense.

> Harold spent as much time on this project as *they did.*
> Harold spent as much time on this project as *he spent on them.*

The first sentence makes more sense, so *they* would be the correct choice.

> Duane can build cabinets better than *I can.*
> Duane can build cabinets better than *he can build me.*

The first sentence makes more sense, so *I* is the correct pronoun.

> The long day exhausted us more than *they did.*
> The long day exhausted us more than *it did them.*

The second sentence makes more sense, so *them* is the correct choice.

> My youngest child is now taller than *I am.*

There is no way to complete the sentence using the pronoun *me*, so *I* is the correct choice.

Pronoun choice is especially important if the sentence makes sense either way. The following sentence can be completed using both pronouns, either of which makes good sense. The pronoun choice controls the meaning. The writer must be careful to choose the correct pronoun if the meaning is to be accurately portrayed.

> I work with Assad more than (she, her).
> I work with Assad more than *she does.*
> I work with Assad more than *I work with her.*

Use the pronoun that portrays the intended meaning.

AMBIGUOUS PRONOUN REFERENCES

Sometimes a sentence is written in such a way that a pronoun can refer to more than one antecedent. When this happens, we say the meaning is *ambiguous*. In the following examples, the ambiguous pronouns are italicized, and the possible antecedents are underlined.

> When <u>Eric</u> spoke to his girlfriend's <u>father</u>, *he* was very polite.
> Remove the <u>door</u> from the <u>frame</u> and paint *it*.
> <u>Jamie</u> told <u>Linda</u> *she* should be ready to go within an hour.
> <u>Pat</u> told <u>Craig</u> *he* had been granted an interview.

See how the sentences are rewritten below to clarify the ambiguous references.

> Eric was very polite when he spoke to his girlfriend's father.
> Paint the door after removing it from the frame.
> Jamie told Linda to be ready to go within an hour.
> Pat told Craig that Craig had been granted an interview.

IMPROPER REFLEXIVE PRONOUNS

A reflexive pronoun is one that includes the word *self* or *selves*: *myself, yourself, himself, herself, ourselves, themselves*. The following section explains ways in which reflexive pronouns are sometimes misused.

- The possessive pronouns *his* and *their* cannot be made reflexive.
  Wrong:
  > They decided to do the remodeling theirselves.
  > Mark wanted to arrange the meeting hisself.

  Correct:
  > They decided to do the remodeling *themselves*.
  > Mark wanted to arrange the meeting *himself*.

- Avoid using a reflexive pronoun when a personal pronoun works in the sentence.
  Wrong:
  > Three associates and myself chose the architect for the building.
  > The preliminary results of the poll were revealed only to ourselves.

  Correct:
  > Three associates and *I* chose the architect for the building.
  > The preliminary results of the poll were revealed only to *us*.

Skill Building Until Next Time

Identify the pronoun mistake or two that you make most often. In your conversation, make a conscious effort to use the pronouns correctly at least three times.

ANSWERS

1. her
2. his
3. his
4. he

5. herself
6. it
7. her
8. his

9. her
10. his, he
11. he, me
12. he

13. I
14. him, me
15. her, them
16. I

PROBLEM VERBS AND PRONOUNS

14

LESSON SUMMARY

Sit or *set*? *Your* or *you're*? *There* or *their*? Or is it *they're*? Knowing how to use such problem pairs is the mark of the educated writer. This lesson shows you how.

T his lesson covers problem verbs such as *lie/lay*, *sit/set*, *rise/raise*, and their various forms. It also covers problem pronouns such as *its/it's*, *your/you're*, *whose/who's*, *who/that/which*, and *there/they're/their*. You can distinguish yourself as an educated writer if you can use these verbs and pronouns correctly in formal writing situations.

PROBLEM VERBS

LIE/LAY

Few people use *lie* and *lay* and their principal parts correctly, perhaps because few people know the difference in meaning between the two. The verb *lie* means *to rest or recline*. The verb *lay* means *to put or place*. The table on the next page shows the principal parts of each of these verbs. Their meanings, written in the correct form, appear in parentheses.

FORMS OF *LIE* AND *LAY*

Present	Progressive	Past	Past Participle*
lie, lies	lying	lay	lain
(rest, rests)	(resting)	(rested)	(rested)
lay, lays	laying	laid	laid
(place, places)	(placing)	(placed)	(placed)

The past participle is the form used with have, has, *or* had.

To choose the correct form of *lie* or *lay*, simply look at the meanings in parentheses. Choose the word in parentheses that makes the most sense and use the corresponding form of *lie* or *lay*. Sometimes none of the words seem especially appropriate. Nevertheless, choose the option that makes more sense than any of the others. If a sentence contains the word *down*, mentally delete the word from the sentence to make the appropriate verb more obvious. Examine the sample sentences to see how this is done.

The garbage cans are _____ in the middle of the street. [Requires progressive]
Resting makes better sense than *placing*.
Choose *lying*.

Keith told Nan to _____ the mail on the dining room table. [Requires present]
Place makes better sense than *rest*.
Choose *lay*.

The sandwiches _____ in the sun for over an hour before we ate them. [Requires past]
Rested makes better sense than *placed*.
Choose *lay*.

Yesterday afternoon, I _____ down for an hour. [Requires past]
Remove the word *down*.
Rested makes better sense than *placed*.
Choose *lay*.

Barry thought he had _____ the papers near the copy machine. [Requires past participle]
Placed makes better sense than *rested*.
Choose *laid*.

PRACTICE

Write the correct form of *lie* or *lay* in each of the blanks below. Answers can be found at the end of the lesson.

1. After the alarm sounded, I _____ in bed for another hour.

2. _____ the packages on the mailroom floor.

3. The latest edition of the newspaper _____ on the desk.

4. The paper carrier _____ the latest edition of the newspaper on the desk.

5. No one had any idea how long the sandwiches had _____ in the sun or who had _____ them there in the first place.

SIT/SET

These two verbs are very similar to *lie* and *lay*. *Sit* means "to rest." *Set* means "to put or place." The table below shows the principal parts of each of these verbs. Their meanings, written in the correct form, appear in parentheses.

FORMS OF *SIT* AND *SET*			
Present	**Progressive**	**Past**	**Past Participle***
sit, sits	sitting	sat	sat
(rest, rests)	(resting)	(rested)	(rested)
set, sets	setting	set	set
(put, place; puts, places)	(putting, placing)	(put, placed)	(put, placed)

The past participle is the form used with have, has, *or* had.

Choose the correct form of *sit* or *set* by using the meanings (the words in parentheses) in the sentence first. Decide which meaning makes the most sense, and then choose the corresponding verb. See how this is done in the example sentences below.

The speaker _____ the chair next to the podium.
   Put or *placed* makes more sense than *rested*.
   Choose *set*.

The speaker _____ in the chair next to the podium.
   Rested makes more sense than *put* or *placed*.
   Choose *sat*.

PRACTICE

Write the correct form of *sit* or *set* in each of the blanks below. Answers are at the end of the lesson.

6. The board of directors _____ aside additional money for research and development.

7. My desk is the one _____ closest to the fax machine.

8. I can't remember where I _____ the mail down.

9. I _____ down next to Jill and _____ my briefcase on the chair next to me.

10. We had _____ in the waiting room for almost an hour before the doctor saw us.

RISE/RAISE

The verb *rise* means "to go up." The verb *raise* means "to move something up." *Raise* requires an object. In other words, something must receive the action of the verb raise (*raise your hand, raise the flag, raise the objection, raise children*). The table below shows the principal parts of both verbs.

FORMS OF *RISE* AND *RAISE*			
Present	**Progressive**	**Past**	**Past Participle***
rises, rise	rising	rose	risen
(goes up, go up)	(going up)	(went up)	(gone up)
(comes up, come up)	(coming up)	(came up)	(come up)
raises, raise	raising	raised	raised
(moves up, move up)	(moving up)	(moved up)	(moved up)

*The past participle is the form used with have, has, *or* had.

Choose the correct form of *rise* or *raise* by using the meanings (the words in parentheses) in the sentence first. Decide which meaning makes the most sense, and choose the corresponding verb. See how this is done in the example sentences below. Sometimes none of the words seem especially appropriate. Nevertheless, choose the option that makes more sense than any of the others.

The sun _____ a little bit earlier each day of the spring.
    Comes up makes the most sense.
    Choose *rises*.

Without realizing it, we began to _____ our voices.
    Move up makes more sense than any of the other options.
    Choose *raise.*

The river _____ over two feet in the last hour.
    Went up makes the most sense.
    Choose *rose.*

PRACTICE

Write the correct form of *rise* or *raise* in each of the blanks below. Answers are at the end of the lesson.

11. The guard _____ the flag every morning before the sun _____.

12. The couple _____ seven of their own children and adopted three more.

13. By late morning the fog had _____ enough for us to see the neighboring farm.

14. The stockholders _____ from their chairs to _____ an objection.

PROBLEM PRONOUNS

ITS/IT'S

Its is a possessive pronoun that means *belonging to it. It's* is a contraction for *it is* or *it has.* The only time you will ever use *it's* is when you can also substitute the words *it is.* Take time to make this substitution, and you will never confuse these two words.

    A doe will hide **its** [belonging to the it—the doe] fawn carefully before going out to graze.
    It's [it is] time we packed up and moved to a new location.
    The new computer system has proven **its** [belonging to it] value.
    We'll leave the game as soon as **it's** [it is] over.

YOUR/YOU'RE

Your is a possessive pronoun that means *belonging to you. You're* is a contraction for the words *you are.* The only time you will ever use *you're* is when you can also substitute the words *you are.* Take time to make this substitution, and you will never confuse these two words.

    Is this **your** [belonging to you] idea of a joke?
    As soon as **you're** [you are] finished, you may leave.

Your [belonging to you] friends are the people you most enjoy.

You're [you are] friends whom we value.

WHOSE/WHO'S

Whose is a possessive pronoun that means *belonging to whom*. *Who's* is a contraction for the words *who is* or *who has*. Take time to make this substitution, and you will never confuse these two words.

Who's [Who is] in charge of the lighting for the show?

Whose [belonging to whom] car was that?

This is the nurse **who's** [who is] on duty until morning.

Here is the man **whose** [belonging to whom] car I ran into this morning.

WHO/THAT/WHICH

Who refers to people. *That* refers to things. *Which* is generally used to introduce nonrestrictive clauses that describe things. (See Lesson 4 for nonrestrictive clauses.) Look at the following sentences to see how each of these words is used.

There is the woman **who** helped me fix my flat tire.

The man **who** invented the polio vaccine died in 1995.

This is the house **that** Jack built.

The book **that** I wanted is no longer in print.

Abigail, **who** rescued my cat from the neighbor's tree, lives across the street.

Yassir Arafat, **who** heads the PLO, met with Israeli leaders.

The teacher asked us to read *Lord of the Flies*, **which** is my favorite novel.

Mt. Massive, **which** is the tallest peak in the Rocky Mountains, looms above Leadville, Colorado.

THERE/THEIR/THEY'RE

There is an adverb telling where an action or item is located. *Their* is a possessive pronoun that shows ownership. *They're* is a contraction for the words *they are*. Of all the confusing word groups, this one is misused most often. Here is an easy way to distinguish among these words.

- Take a close look at this version of the word: t**HERE**. You can see that *there* contains the word *here*. Wherever you use the word *there*, you should be able to substitute the word *here*, and the sentence should still make sense.
- *Their* means *belonging to them*. Of the three words, *their* can be most easily transformed into the word *them*. Try it. You'll discover that two short markings—connecting the *i* to the *r* and then drawing a line to make the *ir* into an *m*—will turn *their* into *them*. This clue will help you avoid misusing *their*.
- Finally, imagine that the apostrophe in *they're* is actually a very small letter *a*. If you change *they're* to *they are* in a sentence, you'll never misuse the word. Look over the example sentences on the next page.

There [here] is my paycheck.

The new chairs are in **there** [here].

Their [belonging to them] time has almost run out.

This is **their** [belonging to them] problem, not mine.

They're [they are] planning to finish early in the morning.

I wonder how **they're** [they are] going to work this out.

PRACTICE

Circle the correct word in each set of parentheses below. Answers are at the end of the lesson.

15. Finally, the dog stopped (its, it's) barking.

16. Alert me when (its, it's) time to go.

17. (Its, It's) time to get a new clock when the old one stops (its, it's) chiming.

18. Take (your, you're) time with this decision.

19. Take (your, you're) samples with you if (your, you're) leaving.

20. (Your, You're) scheduled to work late this evening.

21. (Your, You're) schedule for this evening has changed.

22. My aunt Sophie is the one (who, which, that) travels for a living.

23. This is the book (who, which, that) I lost earlier this year.

24. Kirk Douglas, (who, which, that) is my favorite actor, finally received an Oscar nomination.

25. Redbird Creek, (who, which, that) runs through my back yard, floods every spring.

26. There's the person (who, which, that) gave me directions to the museum.

27. (Your, You're) likely to find the tapes in (there, their, they're).

28. (There, Their, They're) scheduled to begin construction next week.

29. (Its, It's) been over an hour since (there, their, they're) food arrived.

30. The clerk (who, which, that) gave me the estimate is over (there, their, they're).

31. (Who's, Whose) been opening the store in the morning?

32. (Who's, Whose) responsibility is it to open the store in the morning?

33. Hilda spoke to the person (who's, whose) in charge of electronics.

34. (Who's, Whose) birthday is it?

Skill Building Until Next Time

Identify the special verb or pronoun problem that gives you the most trouble. Explain the correct way to use it to a friend or family member. Make a conscious effort to use it correctly at least three times today.

ANSWERS

1. lay	**12.** raised	**24.** who
2. Lay	**13.** risen	**25.** which
3. lay	**14.** rose, raise	**26.** who
4. laid	**15.** its	**27.** You're, there
5. lain, laid	**16.** it's	**28.** They're
6. set	**17.** It's, its	**29.** It's, their
7. sitting	**18.** your	**30.** who, there
8. set	**19.** your, you're	**31.** Who's
9. sat, set	**20.** You're	**32.** Whose
10. sat	**21.** Your	**33.** who's
11. raised, rose	**22.** who	**34.** Whose
or raises, rises	**23.** that	

L·E·S·S·O·N

MODIFIERS

15

LESSON SUMMARY

This lesson shows you how to avoid common problems with adjectives and adverbs.

Words and phrases that describe other words are called *modifiers*. Words that describe nouns and pronouns are called *adjectives*. Words that describe verbs, adjectives, or adverbs are called *adverbs*. Entire phrases or groups of words can also function as modifiers. The English language is structured in such a way that modifiers play a vital part in communication. Using them correctly is an important skill.

ADJECTIVES

Adjectives describe a noun or pronoun in a sentence. Here is an easy way to tell if a word is an adjective. Adjectives answer one of three questions about another word in the sentence: *which one? what kind?* and *how many?* The table on the next page illustrates this. The adjectives are highlighted to make them easy to identify.

ADJECTIVES		
Which One?	**What Kind?**	**How Many?**
that cubicle	**sports** car	**many** examples
the **other** arrangement	**red** stickers	**three** containers
our **first** project	**wise** mentor	**several** desks

Pay special attention to adjectives that follow linking verbs. Sometimes the adjective follows a verb, but it describes a noun or pronoun that comes before the verb. The following sentences illustrate this. The italicized adjectives describe the underlined nouns.

This <u>cheesecake</u> tastes *delicious*. [delicious cheesecake]

Chris's <u>change</u> of heart seemed *appropriate*. [appropriate change]

The <u>room</u> smelled *strange*. [strange room]

FEWER/LESS, NUMBER/AMOUNT

Use the adjective *fewer* to modify plural nouns, things that can be counted. Use *less* for singular nouns that represent a quantity or a degree. Most nouns to which an *s* can be added require the adjective *fewer*.

The promotional staff had **fewer** innovative ideas [plural noun] than the marketing staff.

The marketing staff had **less** time [singular noun] to brainstorm than the promotional staff.

The same principle applies to the nouns *number* and *amount*. Use the noun *number* when referring to things that can be made plural, that can be counted. Use the noun *amount* when referring to nouns that are singular.

The **number** of hours [plural noun] we have for this telethon has been reduced.

The **amount** of time [singular noun] we have for this telethon has been reduced.

ADVERBS

Use adverbs to describe verbs, adjectives, and other adverbs. Here is an easy way to tell if a word is an adverb. Adverbs answer one of these questions about another word in the sentence: *where? when? how?* and *to what extent?* The table below illustrates this. The adverbs are highlighted.

ADVERBS			
Where?	**When?**	**How?**	**To What Extent?**
The line moved **forward**.	I saw him **yesterday**.	They spoke **softly**.	I could **hardly** understand.
Store your gear **below**.	Come around **later**.	Cindy types **quickly**.	You **narrowly** missed that car.
Stand **here**.	We'll talk **tonight**.	He sang **happily**.	We **still** won't give in.

This next table shows examples of adverbs modifying verbs, adjectives, and other adverbs. The adverbs are highlighted; the words they modify are underlined.

ADVERBS THAT MODIFY		
Verbs	**Adjectives**	**Other Adverbs**
Mail arrives **regularly.**	an **extremely** exciting time	**most** cleverly presented
Doves sing **mournfully.**	a **hopelessly** difficult problem	**quite** calmly answered
I responded **immediately.**	an **unusually** sound approach	declined **quite** dramatically

ADJECTIVE OR ADVERB?

Sometimes writers mistakenly use adjectives in the place of adverbs. This is illustrated in the sentences below. The italicized words are adjectives incorrectly used in place of adverbs. The adverb form follows the sentence.

Megan can think of answers very *quick*. [**quickly**]

Store these antiques very *careful*. [**carefully**]

Ernie whispered the news as *quiet* as he could. [**quietly**]

Take special care to choose the correct word when using verbs that deal with the senses: *feel, taste, look, smell, sound*. If the word following the verb describes a noun or pronoun that comes before the verb, use an adjective. On the other hand, if the word following the verb describes the verb, use an adverb. In the table below, the adjectives and adverbs are highlighted and the nouns or verbs they modify are underlined.

MODIFIERS WITH "SENSE" VERBS	
Adjectives	**Adverbs**
The entire group felt **sick** after lunch.	The massage therapist felt **gently** along the patient's spine.
The new keyboard looked **strange** to me.	The detective looked **carefully** at the evidence gathered by the pathologist.
The explanation sounded **plausible** to us.	The biologist smelled the container **gingerly.**

GOOD AND WELL

Good is an adjective. *Well* is an adverb. Sometimes *good* is mistakenly used to describe a verb. Use *well* to describe an action. The words modified by *good* and *well* are underlined in the examples below.

Brenton did **well** on the test.

Raul felt **good** after the marathon.

The new marketing strategy was **well** <u>planned</u>.

The <u>lasagna</u> smelled **good** when I walked through the door.

COMPARISONS

Adjectives and adverbs change form when they are used in comparisons. When you compare two items, use the *comparative* form of the modifier. If you are comparing more than two items, use the *superlative* form of the modifier.

The comparative form is created in one of two ways:

1. Add -*er* to the modifier if it is a short word of one or two syllables.

2. Place the word *more* or the word *less* before the modifier if it is a multisyllable word.

In addition, some modifiers change form completely. Examine the samples in the table below. The first six lines of the table illustrate these special modifiers that change form. The rest use the two rules above.

MODIFIERS IN COMPARISONS		
Modifier	**Comparitive (for two items)**	**Superlative (more than two)**
good	better	best
well	better	best
many	more	most
much	more	most
bad	worse	worst
little	less or lesser	least
neat	neater	neatest
lovely	lovelier	loveliest
funny	funnier	funniest
extreme	more [or less] extreme	most [or least] extreme
intelligent	more [or less] intelligent	most [or least] intelligent
precisely	more [or less] precisely	most [or least] precisely

When comparing items in a prepositional phrase, use *between* for two items, *among* for three or more. Look at how the comparative and superlative forms are used in the following sentences.

Up is the **better** direction for the stock market to be going. [comparing two directions]

Blue looks **better** than any other color we've seen. [comparing two colors many times]

The Buick Park Avenue is the **best** luxury car available. [comparing more than two cars]

The Mississippi is the **best** river for walleye fishing. [comparing more than two rivers]

The first run model was **more thoroughly** tested than the prototype. [comparing two things]

AVOID ILLOGICAL OR UNCLEAR COMPARISONS

"Ellie is more disorganized than any woman," is an illogical statement. It implies that Ellie, who is a woman, is more disorganized than herself. Always include the words *other* or *else* to keep your comparisons from being illogical.

Ellie is more disorganized than any **other** woman.

Ted can concentrate better than anyone **else** in our division.

AVOID DOUBLE COMPARISONS

A double comparison occurs when a writer uses both -*er* or -*est* and *more* or *most*.

DOUBLE COMPARISONS

Wrong	Correct
Diane is the most friendliest person I know.	Diane is the friendliest person I know.
Judi is less sleepier than I am.	Judi is less sleepy than I am.
The writing in this sample seems more plainer than the writing in the other sample.	The writing in this sample seems plainer than the writing in the other sample.

AVOID DOUBLE NEGATIVES

When a negative word is added to a statement that is already negative, a double negative results. Avoid double negatives in your writing. The words *hardly* and *barely* can cause problems; they function as negative words. In the example sentences below, the negative words are highlighted. Pay close attention to how the incorrect sentences are rewritten to avoid the double negative.

DOUBLE NEGATIVES

Wrong	Correct
The warehouse **doesn't** have **no** surplus stock at this time.	The warehouse has **no** surplus stock at this time. The warehouse **doesn't** have any surplus stock at this time.
I **can't hardly** understand this financial report.	I can **hardly** understand this financial report. I **can't** understand this financial report.
The cash on hand **won't barely** cover this expense.	The cash on hand will **barely** cover this expense. The cash on hand **won't** cover this expense.

MISPLACED AND DANGLING MODIFIERS

MISPLACED MODIFIERS

Place words, phrases, or clauses that describe nouns and pronouns as closely as possible to the words they describe. Failure to do this often results in a misplaced modifier—and a sentence that means something other than what was intended.

Words

For example, the words *only, almost,* and *just* should be placed as closely as possible to the word described. The best place is right before the words they describe. The placement of the word affects the meaning of the sentence.

> The customers **only** looked at two samples.
> The customers looked at **only** two samples.

In the first sentence above, the customers "only looked" at the samples; they didn't touch them. In the second sentence, the customers looked at "only two," not three or four, samples. The placement of *only* changes the meaning.

Here's an example with *almost:*

> Chad **almost** scored three touchdowns.
> Chad scored **almost** three touchdowns.

In the first version, Chad "almost scored" three times—he must have come close to the goal line three times without actually crossing. In the second version, Chad scored "almost three" touchdowns—maybe 2.2 touchdowns. How many points are awarded for that?

Here's how placing *just* can affect the meaning of a sentence:

> The Hill family **just** leases a car.
> The Hill family leases **just** a car.

In the first version, the Hill family "just leases" a car, so they don't own or buy a car. In the second, they lease "just a car," not a truck or a van or any other vehicle.

Phrases and Clauses

Phrases and clauses that describe nouns or pronouns must also be placed as closely as possible to the words they describe. The following sentences contain misplaced modifiers. Pay close attention to how they are rewritten to clarify the meaning.

MISPLACED MODIFIERS

Wrong	Correct
The veterinarian explained how to vaccinate hogs in the community center basement. [Why would you want hogs in the community center?]	In the community center basement, the veterinarian explained how to vaccinate hogs. The veterinarian in the community center basement explained how to vaccinate hogs.
A big dog followed the old man that was barking loudly. [Why was the man barking?]	A big dog that was barking loudly followed the old man. Barking loudly, a big dog followed the old man.

DANGLING MODIFIERS

Words, phrases, or clauses that begin a sentence and are set off by commas sometimes mistakenly modify the wrong noun or pronoun. These are called dangling modifiers. The following sentences contain dangling modifiers. Pay close attention to how the sentences are rewritten to avoid the problem.

DANGLING MODIFIERS

Wrong	Correct
Flat and useless, Jason removed the bicycle tire. [Why was Jason flat?]	Jason removed the flat and useless bicycle tire. Flat and useless, the bicycle tire was removed by Jason.
Attached to an old stump, Janette saw a No Fishing sign. [Why was Janette attached to an old stump?]	Janette saw a No Fishing sign attached to an old stump. The No Fishing sign attached to an old stump caught Janette's attention.
While cleaning up after dinner, the phone rang. [Don't you wish you had a phone that cleaned up after dinner?]	While I was cleaning up after dinner, the phone rang. While cleaning up after dinner, I heard the phone ring. The phone rang while I was cleaning up after dinner.

PRACTICE

Circle the correct word in each of the following sentences. The answers to this set of questions can be found at the end of the lesson.

1. Greg assembled the desk (correct, correctly).

2. Charlotte seemed (tired, tiredly) after the long plane ride.

3. This drawer doesn't open as (easy, easily) as it used to.

4. My new shoes feel more (comfortable, comfortably) than my old ones.

5. Make your request (polite, politely) if you want a positive response.

6. The workers walked (slow, slowly) back to the line after the break.

7. Our team leader seemed (unhappy, unhappily) about something.

8. The passenger on the other side of the bus looked (angry, angrily).

9. The night watchman felt (careful, carefully) for the switch.

10. We looked (thorough, thoroughly) in both locations.

11. You'll have (fewer, less) trouble with this component if you use (fewer, less) joints.

12. The (number, amount) of people we hire will depend on the (number, amount) of time we have to fill the order.

13. Spaghetti tastes especially (good, well) if the noodles are boiled (good, well).

14. Kelly is the (older, oldest) of the twins and the (taller, tallest) one in the whole family.

15. The receiving department hasn't heard (anything, nothing) about the delivery date of our order.

16. Divide these cookies (between, among) the twins, but split the cake (between, among) all the people who come to the party.

Choose the correctly written sentence from each of the following sets.

17. a. I like olives and pimentoes boiled in oil.
  b. Boiled in oil, I like olives and pimentos.

18. a. While speeding along a country road, two deer dashed across the road in front of our car.
  b. Two deer dashed across the road in front of our car as we were speeding along a country road.

19. a. At the age of four, my grandmother taught me to read.
  b. When I was four, my grandmother taught me to read.

20. a. We heard about the bank robbers who were arrested on the evening news.
  b. We heard on the evening news about the bank robbers who were arrested.

Skill Building Until Next Time

Practice what you have learned in this lesson by listening to others speak. Many people make mistakes with modifiers as they speak. When you hear such a mistake, think about how you might rephrase what the person said to make it correct. Once again, don't feel compelled to correct the mistakes; just use them as opportunities for mental practice so that no one will have the opportunity to correct *you*.

ANSWERS

1. correctly
2. tired
3. easily
4. comfortable
5. politely
6. slowly
7. unhappy
8. angry
9. carefully
10. thoroughly

11. less, fewer
12. number, amount
13. good, well
14. older, tallest
15. anything
16. between, among
17. a.
18. b.
19. b.
20. b.

L·E·S·S·O·N

EASILY CONFUSED WORD PAIRS

16

LESSON SUMMARY

Threw or *through? To, two,* or *too? Brake* or *break?* This lesson and the next one review a host of words that are often confused with other words and show you when to use them.

his lesson covers some of the most commonly confused word pairs, those you are likely to use in your writing. If you learn to distinguish these words, you can avoid errors in your writing. These words are divided into three separate sections with practice exercises at the end of each section. The italicized words following some of the entries are synonyms, words that can be substituted in a sentence for the easily confused words.

THREE-WAY CONFUSION

LEAD/LED/LEAD

- **Lead** as a verb means *guide, direct.* As a noun, it means *front position.* It rhymes with *seed.*
- **Led** is a verb, the past tense of **lead**, meaning *guided, directed.* It rhymes with *red.*
- **Lead** is a noun that is *the name of a metal.* It rhymes with *red.*

Examples:

Geronimo **led** (*guided*) the small band to safety.

We hope the next elected officials will **lead** (*guide*) us to economic recovery.

A pound of styrofoam weighs as much as a pound of **lead** (*the metal*).

Jake took the **lead** (*front position*) as the group headed out of town.

QUITE/QUIT/QUIET

- **Quite** is an adverb meaning *completely, very, entirely*. It rhymes with *fight*.
- **Quit** is a verb meaning *stop, cease* or *stopped, ceased*. It rhymes with *sit*.
- **Quiet** as an adjective means *calm, silent, noiseless*. As a verb, it means *soothe, calm*. As a noun, it means *tranquility, peacefulness*. It almost rhymes with *riot*.

Example:

The firm was **quite** (*very*) surprised when its most productive investment specialist **quit** (*stopped*) work and opted for the **quiet** (*calm*) life of a monk.

RIGHT/WRITE/RITE

- **Right** is an adjective meaning *correct, proper, opposite of left*.
- **Write** is a verb meaning *record, inscribe*.
- **Rite** is a noun meaning *ceremony, ritual*.

Example:

I will **write** (*record*) the exact procedures so you will be able to perform the **rite** (*ceremony*) in the **right** (*proper*) way.

SENT/CENT/SCENT

- **Sent** is a verb, the past tense of *send*. It means *dispatched, transmitted*.
- **Cent** is a noun meaning *one penny*, a coin worth .01 of a dollar.
- **Scent** is a noun meaning *odor, smell*.

Example:

For a mere **cent** (*penny*) I bought an envelope perfumed with the **scent** (*odor*) of jasmine. I **sent** (*dispatched*) it to my grandmother.

SIGHT/SITE/CITE

- **Sight** as a noun means *ability to see*. As a verb, it means *see, spot*.
- **Site** is a noun meaning *location, position*.
- **Cite** is a verb meaning *quote, make reference to*.

Example:

At ninety-five my grandmother's **sight** (*ability to see*) was acute enough to **sight** (*spot*) even the smallest error in a crocheted doily.

This is the proposed **site** (*location*) for the new building.

You must **cite** (*make reference to*) the source of your information.

TO/TOO/TWO

- **To** is a preposition or part of an infinitive. Use it only to introduce a prepositional phrase, which usually answers the question *where*, or before a verb. Use **to** for introducing a prepositional phrase: *to the store, to the top, to my home, to our garden, to his laboratory, to his castle, to our advantage, to an open door, to the science room*, etc. Use **to** as an infinitive (*to* followed by a verb, sometimes separated by adverbs): *to run, to jump, to want badly, to seek, to propose, to write, to explode, to sorely need, to badly botch, to carefully examine*, etc.
- **Too** is an adverb meaning *also, very*.
- **Two** is an adjective, *the name of a number*, as in one, two, three.

Example:

The couple went **to** (*preposition*) the deli **to** (*infinitive*) pick up **two** (*the number*) plate dinners because both of them were **too** (*very*) tired **to** (*infinitive*) cook dinner.

WHERE/WEAR/WERE

- **Where** is an adverb referring to *place, location*.
- **Wear** as a verb means *put on, tire*. As a noun, it means *deterioration*.
- **Were** is a verb, the plural past tense of *be*.

Examples:

The slacks **were** (*form of be*) too tight.

The tires showed excessive **wear** (*deterioration*).

They will **wear** (*tire*) out these shoes if they **wear** (*put on*) them too much.

Where (*location*) are the clothes you **were** (*form of be*) planning to **wear** (*put on*) tomorrow?

PRACTICE

Circle the correct word in the parentheses below. Answers can be found at the end of the lesson.

1. The package will be (sent, cent, scent) if you add another (sent, cent, scent) of postage.

2. We noticed the distinct (sent, cent, scent) of cat litter when we entered the door.

3. Was I (right, write, rite) in assuming I was to (right, write, rite) you a memo about this matter?

4. Who will be performing the (right, write, rite) of baptism at tomorrow's service?

5. If you will simply be (quite, quit, quiet), I will be (quite, quit, quiet) happy to (quite, quit, quiet) annoying you with my constant request for a (quite, quit, quiet) atmosphere in which to work.

6. Our marching band (lead, led) the parade.

7. The drum major, carrying a baton made of (lead, led), will (lead, led) the band.

8. Over the next ridge we will be able to (sight, site, cite) the (sight, site, cite) we've chosen for our new home.

9. I would be honored to have you (sight, site, cite) me in your research.

10. Even though these trousers (where, wear, were) expensive, they are showing (where, wear, were) along the seams.

11. (Where, wear, were) did you buy those earrings?

EASY MISSES

BRAKE/BREAK

- **Brake** as a verb means *slow, stop.* As a noun, it means *hindrance, drag.*
- **Break** as a verb means *separate, shatter, adjourn.* As a noun, it means *separation, crack, pause, opportunity.*

Examples:

During our **break** (*pause*) we spotted a **break** (*crack*) in the pipeline.

Brake (*slow*) gently when driving on glare ice by applying slight pressure to the **brake** (*drag*).

PASSED/PAST

- **Passed** is a verb, the past tense of *pass,* meaning *transferred, went ahead or by, elapsed, finished.*
- **Past** as a noun means *history.* As an adjective, it means *former.*

Examples:

The first runner **passed** (*transferred*) the baton to the second just as she **passed** (*went by*) the stands. Three seconds **passed** (*elapsed*) before the next runner came by.

Harriet **passed** (*finished*) her bar exam on the first try.

I must have been a whale in a **past** (*former*) life.

Avoid digging up the **past** (*history*) if you can.

PEACE/PIECE

- **Peace** is a noun meaning *tranquility.*
- **Piece** as a noun means *division, creation.* As a verb, it means *patch, repair.*

Example:

If you can **piece** (*patch*) together the **pieces** (*bits*) of this story, perhaps we can have some **peace** (*tranquility*) around here.

PLAIN/PLANE

- **Plain** as an adjective means *ordinary, clear, simple.* As a noun, it refers to *flat country,* also sometimes written as **plains.**
- **Plane** is a noun meaning *airship* or *flat surface.* It is occasionally used as a verb or adjective meaning *level.*

Examples:

They wore **plain** (*ordinary)* clothes.

It was **plain** (*clear*) to see.

The meal we ate on the **plains** (*flat country*) was quite **plain** (*simple*).

It was **plain** (*clear*) to us that the enemy did not see our **plane** (*airship*) sitting on the open **plain** (*flat country*).

SCENE/SEEN

- **Scene** is a noun meaning *view, site, commotion.*
- **Seen** is a verb, the past participle of *see,* meaning *observed, noticed.*

Example:

We caused quite a **scene** (*commotion*) at the **scene** (*site*) of the accident. It was the worst we had ever **seen** (*observed*).

THREW/THROUGH

- **Threw** is a verb, the past tense of *throw,* meaning *tossed.*
- **Through** is an adverb or a preposition meaning *in one side and out the other.* Use **through** to introduce a prepositional phrase: *through the door, through the lobby, though the mist.*

Example:

Fred **threw** (*tossed*) the ball **through** (*in one side and out the other*) the hoop.

WEAK/WEEK

- **Weak** is an adjective meaning *flimsy, frail, powerless.*
- **Week** is a noun meaning *a period of seven days.*

Example:

The patient's heartbeat was so **weak** (*frail*) that the doctor was certain he would be dead within a **week** (*seven days*).

WHICH/WITCH

- **Which** is a pronoun dealing with *choice*. As an adverb, it introduces a subordinate clause.
- **Witch** is a noun meaning *sorceress, enchantress*.

Examples:

Which (*choice*) one do you want?

This car, **which** (*introduces subordinate clause*) I have never driven, is the one I'm thinking about buying.

I don't know **which** (*choice*) **witch** (*enchantress*) I should consult about my future.

PRACTICE

Circle the correct word in the parentheses below. Answers can be found at the end of the lesson.

12. (Which, Witch) (which, witch) scares you the most?

13. Gerald (threw, through) away his opportunity when he walked (threw, through) the door.

14. Sally slammed on the (brake, break) when she saw the car ahead (brake, break) to avoid the (brake, break) in the concrete road.

15. Have you (scene, seen) that pathetic (scene, seen) in the movie?

16. The confused (which, witch) couldn't decide (which, witch) broomstick to use on Halloween.

17. The sales department has (passed, past) the record it had established in the (passed, past) year.

18. We'll need at least a (weak, week) to repair the (weak, week) linkage in this machine.

19. This (peace, piece) of news should give you some (peace, piece) of mind.

20. The (plain, plane) brown packages were loaded on the (plain, plane).

TO SPLIT OR NOT TO SPLIT

ALREADY/ALL READY

- **Already** is an adverb meaning *as early as this, previously, by this time*.
- **All ready** means *completely ready, totally ready*.

Examples:

At age four, Brigitta is reading **already** (*as early as this*).

We had **already** (*previously, by this time*) finished.

Are we **all ready** (*completely ready*) to go?

ALTOGETHER/ALL TOGETHER

- **Altogether** is an adverb meaning *entirely, completely.*
- **All together** means *simultaneously.*

Examples:

These claims are **altogether** (*entirely*) false.

The audience responded **all together** (*simultaneously*).

EVERYDAY/EVERY DAY

- **Everyday** is an adjective meaning *ordinary, usual.*
- **Every day** means *each day.*

Examples:

These are our **everyday** (*usual*) low prices.

The associates sort the merchandise **every day** (*each day*).

MAYBE/MAY BE

- **Maybe** is an adverb meaning *perhaps.*
- **May be** is a verb phrase meaning *might be.*

Example:

Maybe (*perhaps*) the next batch will be better than this one. On the other hand, it **may be** (*might be*) worse.

ALWAYS SPLIT

- **All right.** There's no such word as *alright,* though you will sometimes see it written this way.
- **A lot.** There's no such word as *alot.* There's a word *allot,* but it means *to portion out* something.

Example:

I thought it was **all right** that we **allotted** tickets to **a lot** of our best customers.

PRACTICE

Circle the correct word in the parentheses below.

21. I (where, wear, were) my (everyday, every day) clothes almost (everyday, every day).

22. (Maybe, may be) we should design a new model. It (maybe, may be) just the thing to brighten our financial picture.

23. If you had been (already, all ready), we could have (already, all ready) begun.

24. You'll be (alright, all right) if you follow the instructions.

25. When the staff is (altogether, all together), we should have (altogether, all together) enough brainpower for this project.

Skill Building Until Next Time

See how many of these easily confused words you can spot in your reading. Try substituting the synonyms you learned.

ANSWERS

1. sent, cent
2. scent
3. right, write
4. rite
5. quiet, quite, quit, quiet
6. led

7. lead, lead
8. sight, site
9. cite
10. were, wear
11. Where
12. Which, witch
13. threw, through

14. brake, brake, break
15. seen, scene
16. witch, which
17. passed, past
18. week, weak
19. piece, peace
20. plain, plane

21. wear, everyday, every day
22. Maybe, may be
23. all ready, already
24. all right
25. all together, altogether

MORE EASILY CONFUSED WORDS

17

LESSON SUMMARY

Some of the most commonly used words in the English language are easily confused with other equally common words. To avoid confusing readers, you need to know which ones are which.

This lesson covers more of the most commonly confused words pairs, those you are likely to use in your writing. If you learn to distinguish these words, you can avoid errors. The words are divided into three separate sections with practice exercises at the end of each section. The words in italics following some of the entries are synonyms, words that can be substituted in a sentence for the easily confused words.

SMALL BUT TRICKY

BY/BUY

- **By** is a preposition used to introduce a phrase (by the book, by the time, by the way)
- **Buy** as a verb means *purchase*. As a noun, it means *bargain, deal*.
  Examples:
  We stopped **by** *(preposition)* the store to **buy** *(purchase)* some
      groceries.
  That car was a great **buy** *(deal)*.

DEAR/DEER

- **Dear** is an adjective meaning *valued, loved.*
- **Deer** is a noun referring to an *animal,* a four-legged one that lives in the woods and looks like Bambi.
  Example:

  The **dear** *(loved)* man died when his car struck a **deer** *(animal).*

DIE/DYE

- **Die** is a verb meaning *pass away, fade.*
- **Dye** as a verb means to *color, tint.* As a noun, it refers to *coloring, pigment.*
  Example:

  We waited for the wind to **die** *(fade)* before we decided to **dye** *(color)* the sheets.

HEAR/HERE

- **Hear** is a verb meaning *listen to.*
- **Here** is an adverb meaning *in this place, to this place.*
  Example:

  Please come **here** *(to this place)* so you can **hear** *(listen to)* what I have to say.

HOLE/WHOLE

- **Hole** is a noun meaning *opening, gap.*
- **Whole** as an adjective means *entire, intact.* As a noun, it means *entire part or amount.*
  Examples:

  The **whole** *(entire)* group heard the message.

  They patched the **hole** *(opening)* in the wall.

KNEW/NEW

- **Knew** is a verb, the past tense of *know.* It means *understood, recognized.*
- **New** is an adjective meaning *fresh, different, current.*
  Example:

  I **knew** *(understood)* they were planning to buy a **new** *(different)* car.

KNOW/NO

- **Know** is a verb meaning *understand, recognize.*
- **No** as an adverb means *not so, not at all.* As an adjective, it means *none, not one.*
  Example:

  As far as I **know** *(understand),* we have **no** *(not one)* more of these shoes in stock.

MEAT/MEET

- Meat is a noun meaning *food, flesh, main part.*
- Meet as a verb means *assemble, greet, fulfill.* As a noun, it means *assembly.*
  Examples:
  Before a track **meet** *(assembly)*, it is better to eat foods high in carbohydrates rather than **meat** *(flesh)*.
  The **meat** *(main part)* of his message was that our efforts did not **meet** *(fulfill)* his standards.

ONE/WON

- One can be an adjective meaning *single.* It can also be a pronoun used to mean a single person or thing.
- Won is a verb, the past tense of *win.* It means *prevailed, achieved, acquired.*
  Example:
  Jacquez is the **one** *(pronoun referring to Jacquez)* who **won** *(achieved)* the most improved bowler trophy
    this year.

SEAM/SEEM

- Seam is a noun meaning *joint, joining point.*
- Seem is a verb meaning *appear.*
  Example:
  Does it **seem** *(appear)* to you as if this **seam** *(joint)* is weakening?

PRACTICE

Circle the correct word in the parentheses below. Answers can be found at the end of the lesson.

1. If the copier isn't repaired (by, buy) noon, we'll need to (by, buy) a new one.

2. (By, Buy) this book that was written (by, buy) a well-known expert on the subject. It's a great (by, buy).

3. The (dear, deer) I had as a pet was quite (dear, deer) to me.

4. The sound began to (die, dye) during the most exciting part of the movie.

5. How do I (die, dye) this shirt?

6. If you sit (hear, here), you'll be able to (hear, here) much better.

7. We can see the (hole, whole) field through this little (hole, whole).

8. I wish I (knew, new) how to operate this (knew, new) equipment.

9. You (know, no) we have (know, no) idea how to solve this problem.

10. After a kill, a pride of lions will (meat, meet) so each can get a share of the (meat, meet).

11. The Colts (one, won) the game by just (one, won) point.

12. I (seam, seem) to be unable to locate the (seam, seem) in this pipe.

OFTEN USED AND MISUSED

CHOOSE/CHOSE

- **Choose** is a verb meaning *select*. It rhymes with *bruise*.
- **Chose** is past tense of *choose*; it means *selected*. It rhymes with *hose*.
  Example:
      Henry **chose** *(selected)* flex hours on Friday afternoons. I will **choose** *(select)* the same option.

LOOSE/LOSE/LOSS

- **Loose** is an adjective meaning *free, unrestrained, not tight*. It rhymes with *goose*.
- **Lose** is a verb meaning *misplace, to be defeated, fail to keep*. It rhymes with *shoes*.
- **Loss** is a noun meaning *defeat, downturn,* the opposite of *victory* or *gain*. It rhymes with *toss.*
  Examples:
      The chickens ran **loose** *(free)* in the yard.
      The knot holding the boat to the dock was **loose** *(not tight).*
      Where did you **lose** *(misplace)* your gloves?
      The investors will **lose** *(fail to keep)* considerable capital if the market suffers a **loss** *(downturn).*

SUPPOSE/SUPPOSED

- **Suppose** is a verb meaning *assume, imagine.*
- **Supposed** as a verb is the past tense of *suppose* and means *assumed, imagined.* As an adjective it means *expected, obligated.*
  Examples:
      I **suppose** *(assume)* you'll be late, as usual.
      We all **supposed** *(assumed)* you would be late.
      You were **supposed** *(expected)* to have picked up the copies of the report before you came to the meeting.

THAN/THEN

- **Than** is a conjunctive word used to make a comparison.
- **Then** is an adverb telling *when* or meaning *next*.

    Example:

    Then *(next)*, the group discussed the ways in which the new procedures worked better *than (conjunction making a comparison)* the old.

USE/USED

- **Use** as a verb means *utilize, deplete*. It rhymes with *ooze*. As a noun, it rhymes with *goose* and means *purpose*.
- **Used** as a verb is the past tense of *use* and means *utilized, depleted*. As an adjective, it means *second-hand*.
- **Used to** can be used as an adjective, meaning *accustomed to*, or as an adverb meaning *formerly*. (Note that you never write *use to* when you mean *accustomed to* or *formerly*.)

    Examples:

    Just **use** *(utilize)* the same password we **used** *(utilized)* yesterday.

    What's the **use** *(purpose)* in trying yet another time?

    We should consider buying **used** *(second-hand)* equipment.

    We **used to** *(formerly)* require(*d*) a second opinion.

    Residents of Buffalo, New York, are **used to** *(accustomed to)* cold temperatures.

WEATHER/WHETHER

- **Weather** is a noun referring to the *condition outside*.
- **Whether** is adverb used when referring to *a possibility*.

    Examples:

    The **weather** *(condition outside)* took a turn for the worse.

    Let me know **whether** *(a possibility)* you are interested in this new system.

PRACTICE

Circle the correct word in the parentheses below. The answers can be found at the end of the lesson.

13. If you (choose, chose) your words carefully, you can avoid offending anyone else.

14. The committee (choose, chose) the model with the most special features.

15. The (loose, lose, loss) caused the stockholders to (loose, lose, loss) confidence in the company.

16. How could you (loose, lose, loss) your temper over such a trivial matter?

17. The paper tray seems (loose, lose, loss) to me.

18. I (suppose, supposed) you thought I was the one who was (suppose, supposed) to speak at the banquet.

19. Add even more sugar (than, then) you already have, and (than, then) stir the mixture thoroughly.

20. We found yet another (use, used) for the (use, used) tires that (use, used) to be stacked outside the building.

21. Do you know (weather, whether) this beautiful (weather, whether) is (suppose, supposed) to continue into the weekend?

KILLER *A*'S AND *AL*'S

ACCEPT/EXCEPT/EXPECT

- **Accept** is a verb meaning *receive, bear.*
- **Except** is a preposition meaning *but, excluding.*
- **Expect** is a verb meaning *anticipate, demand, assume.*
  Examples:
    This client **expects** *(demands)* nothing **except** *(but)* the most sophisticated options available.
    Will you **accept** *(bear)* the responsibility for this decision?
    We **expect** *(anticipate)* everyone to come **except** *(excluding)* John.

ADVICE/ADVISE

- **Advice** is a noun meaning *suggestion, suggestions.* It rhymes with *ice.* (Hint: Think *adv*ICE.)
- **Advise** is a verb meaning *suggest to, warn.* It rhymes with *wise.*
  Examples:
    We **advise** *(suggest to)* you to proceed carefully.
    That was the best **advice** *(suggestion)* I've received so far.

AFFECT/EFFECT

- **Affect** is a verb meaning *alter, inspire or move emotionally, imitate.* **Affected,** besides being the past tense of *affect,* can also be used as an adjective meaning *imitated, pretentious.*
- **Effect** as a noun means *consequence.* As a verb, it means *cause.*
  Examples:
    How will this plan **affect** *(alter)* our jobs? What **effect** *(consequence)* will this restructuring have on profits? Will it **effect** *(cause)* an increase?
    The movie **affected** *(moved emotionally)* Marian.
    He **affected** *(imitated)* an English accent.
    The **affected** *(pretentious)* speech fooled no one.

CAPITAL/CAPITOL

- **Capital** as a noun means either *assets* or *the city that is the seat of government.* As an adjective, it means *main, very important,* or *deserving of death.*
- **Capitol** is a noun referring to *the building that houses the government.*

  Examples:

  How much **capital** *(assets)* are you willing to invest?

  I think that's a **capital** *(main)* objective.

  First degree murder is a **capital** *(deserving of death)* crime.

  Albany is the **capital** *(city)* of New York.

  No legislators were injured in the explosion in the **capitol** *(building).*

PERSONAL/PERSONNEL

- **Personal** is an adjective meaning *private.*
- **Personnel** is a noun meaning *staff, employees* or an adjective meaning *dealing with staff or employees.*

  Examples:

  The director of **personnel** *(staff)* keeps all the **personnel** *(employee)* files in order and guards any **personal** *(private)* information they contain.

PRINCIPAL/PRINCIPLE

- **Principal** as a noun refers to the *head of a school* or an *investment.* As an adjective, it means *primary, major.*
- **Principle** is a noun meaning *rule, law, belief.*

  Examples:

  The **principal** *(head)* of Calbert High School used the **principal** *(investment)* of an endowment fund to cover this month's salaries.

  The **principal** *(primary)* objective is to make decisions that are in keeping with our **principles** *(beliefs).*

PRACTICE

Circle the correct word in the parentheses below. The answers can be found at the end of the lesson.

22. Surely you didn't (accept, except, expect) Weldon to (accept, except, expect) responsibility for this decision when everyone (accept, except, expect) him was consulted.

23. We (accept, except, expect) the delivery to arrive early in the morning.

24. The soothsayer will (advice, advise) you to seek her (advice, advise) often.

25. The new work schedule (affected, effected) production in a positive way.

26. How will this new work schedule (affect, effect) production?

27. What (affect, effect) will this new work schedule have on production?

28. We plan to tour the (capital, capitol) building whenever we visit a state's (capital, capitol) city.

29. We never release (personal, personnel) information about our (personal, personnel).

30. The employees' (principal, principle) concern is workload.

31. The new legislation violates the basic (principals, principles) upon which the country was founded.

Skill Building Until Next Time

Make a conscious effort to use the correct forms of these easily confused words in your writing. You may find it helpful to copy the words and their synonyms onto a separate sheet of paper. This will provide a good review and serve as a handy reference you can keep with you as you write.

ANSWERS

1. by, buy	**10.** meet, meat	**19.** than, then	**26.** affect
2. Buy, by, buy	**11.** won, one	**20.** use, used, used	**27.** effect
3. deer, dear	**12.** seem, seam	**21.** whether, weather, supposed	**28.** capitol, capital
4. die	**13.** choose	**22.** expect, accept, except	**29.** personal, personnel
5. dye	**14.** chose	**23.** expect	**30.** principal
6. here, hear	**15.** loss, lose	**24.** advise, advice	**31.** principles
7. whole, hole	**16.** lose	**25.** affected	
8. knew, new	**17.** loose		
9. know, no	**18.** suppose, supposed		

L·E·S·S·O·N

DICTION

18

LESSON SUMMARY

"Diction?" you might think. "In a book about writing?" While *diction* refers to how words are pronounced, it also refers to *which* words you choose. In order to use language effectively, writers have to write concisely and precisely. This lesson and Lesson 19 focus on how to choose the words that best communicate what you want to say.

A word is a terrible thing to waste. Or is it better to say, "It is a terrible thing to waste a word"? The difference between these two versions is a matter of *diction*, using appropriate words and combining them in the right way to communicate your message accurately. This lesson discusses ways to avoid some of the most common diction traps: wordiness, lack of precison, clichés, and jargon. Learning to recognize and avoid such writing weaknesses will turn a mediocre writer into a good one—this means expressing ideas in the *best* and *clearest* way possible.

WORDINESS

Excess words in communication waste space and time. Not only that, but they may also distort the message or make it difficult for the reader to understand. Get in the habit of streamlining your writing, making the sentences as concise as possible. If you use five words where three would do, delete the extra words or structure your sentences to avoid them. See if you can rewrite the sentences in the first column to make them less wordy. Check yourself agains the version in the second column.

Wordy	Revised
It was a three-hour period after the accident when the rescue squad that we knew was going to help us arrived. [21 words]	The rescue squad arrived three hours after the accident. [9 words]
It was decided that the church would organize a committee for the purpose of conducting a search for a new pastor. [21 words]	The church organized a committee to search for a new pastor. [11 words]

The additional words in the first column add no information. All they do is take up space.

BUZZWORDS AND FLUFFY MODIFIERS

Buzzwords such as *aspect, element, factor, scope, situation, type, kind, forms,* and so on sound important, but add no meaning to a sentence. They often signal a writer who has little or nothing to say, yet wishes to sound important. Likewise, modifiers such as *absolutely, definitely, really, very, important, significant, current, major,* and *quite* may add length to a sentence, but they seldom add meaning.

Wordy
The *nature of the* scheduling system is a *very important matter* that can *definitely* have a *really significant* impact on the morale *aspect* of an employee's attitude. *Aspects of* our current scheduling policy make it *absolutely necessary* that we undergo a *significant* change.

Revised
The scheduling system can affect employee morale. Our policy needs to be changed.

The following table lists a host of phrases that can be reduced to one or two words.

Wordy	Concise	Wordy	Concise
puzzling in nature	puzzling	at this point in time	now, today
of a peculiar kind	peculiar	at that point in time	then
regardless of the fact that	although	in order to	to
due to the fact that	because	by means of	by
of an indefinite nature	indefinite	exhibits a tendency to	tends to
concerning the matter of	about	in connection with	with
in the event that	if	in relation to	with

PASSIVE VOICE

Some wordiness is caused by using passive voice verbs when you could use the active voice. (See Lesson 11 if you don't remember passive voice.)

Passive	Active
It has been decided that your application for grant money is not in accordance with the constraints outlined by the committee in the application guidelines.	The committee denied your grant because it did not follow the application guidelines.
The letter of resignation was accepted by the Board of Directors.	The Board of Directors accepted the resignation.

INTELLECTUAL-ESE

The passive sentences above suffer not only from passive voice wordiness, but also from the writer's attempt to make the writing sound intellectual, to make the message more difficult than it needs to be. Writers make this error in many ways. One way is to turn adjectives and verbs into nouns. This transformation usually means that extra words are added to the sentence.

Wordy	Revised
Water *pollution* [noun] is not as serious in the northern parts of Canada.	Water is not as *polluted* [adjective] in northern Canada.
Customer *demand* [noun] is reducing in the area of sales services.	Customers *demand* [verb] fewer sales services.

Another way writers add words without adding meaning is to use a pretentious tone. Below is an actual memo issued by a bureaucrat during World War II. When it was sent to President Franklin Roosevelt for his approval, he edited the memo before sending it on. The original and Roosevelt's edited versions are printed below.

Original pretentious memo:

In the unlikely event of an attack by an invader of a foreign nature, such preparations shall be made as will completely obscure all Federal buildings and non-Federal buildings occupied by the Federal government during an air raid for any period of time from visibility by reason of internal or external illumination.

Roosevelt's revised memo:

If there is an air raid, put something across the windows and turn off the lights outside in buildings where we have to keep the work going.

Here's another example of pretentious writing, along with a clearer revised version.

Pompous memo:

As per the most recent directive issued from this office, it is incumbent upon all employees and they are henceforth instructed to reduce in amount the paper used in the accomplishment of their daily tasks due to the marked increase in the cost of such supplies.

Revised:

Since paper costs have increased, employees must use less paper.

WORD ECONOMY	
Stretched Sentence	**Concise Sentence**
Cassandra seems to be content.	Cassandra seems content.
We must know what it is that we are doing.	We must know what we're doing.
This is the book of which I have been speaking.	I spoke about this book.
It is with pleasure that I announce the winner.	I am pleased to announce the winner.
The reason we were late was because of traffic.	We were late because of traffic.
These plans will be considered on an individual basis.	These plans will be considered individually.
The caterer, who was distressed, left the party.	The distressed caterer left the party.
There are new shipments arriving daily.	New shipments arrive daily.
Due to the fact that we were late, we missed the door prizes.	We came late and missed the door prizes.
The consideration given in the latest promotion is an example of how I was treated unfairly.	I was not fairly considered for the latest promotion.

Writers sometimes stretch their sentences with unnecessary words, all in an effort to sound intelligent. The table on the previous page illustrates stretched sentences have been rewritten more concisely.

REDUNDANCY

Another writing trap that takes up space is redundancy, repeating words that express the same idea or in which the meanings overlap. If you stop to think about phrases like those below—and many others—you'll see that the extra words are not only unnecessary but often just plain silly.

enclosed *with this letter*	continue *on*, proceed *ahead*
remit *payment*	repeated *over again*
absolutely necessary	gather *together*
weather *outside*	*compulsory* requirement
postpone *until later*	*temporarily* suspended
refer *back*	*necessary* requirements
past history	plain *and simple*
ask *the question*	

Enclosed means it's in this letter, doesn't it? *Remit* means *pay*. And how can something be more *necessary* than *necessary*? The weather *outside* as opposed to the weather *inside*? *Past* history as opposed to . . . ? You see the point. Keep it simple. (Not *plain and simple*.)

PRACTICE

Try rewriting the following sentences to remove the fluffy wording. Suggested revisions are at the end of this lesson, but your versions may be different; there's more than one way to rewrite these sentences.

1. Stephanie is a very important employee who has played a significant role in the success of this company.

2. Some educators hold with the opinion that corporal punishment should in fact be reinstated in our schools to act as a deterrent to those students who are considering engaging in inappropriate behavior.

3. It is certainly a true statement that bears repeating over and over again that technological advancements such as computers can assist employees in performing in a very efficient manner, and that these self-same computers may in fact result in considerable savings over a period of time.

4. I arrived at a decision to allow the supervisor of my department to achieve a higher golf score in order to enhance my opportunities for advancement in the event that such opportunities became available.

PRECISE LANGUAGE

Work to make your writing as precise as possible. In doing so, you communicate more meaning using fewer words. In other words, you make your writing more concise. Choose exact verbs, modifiers, and nouns to help you transmit an exact meaning.

IMPRECISE VS. PRECISE

Verbs	
Emilia participated in the protest.	Emilia organized the march on the capital.
Hannah won't deal with sales meetings.	Hannah won't attend sales meetings.
Dick can relate to Jane.	Dick understands Jane's feelings.

Modifiers	
These bad instructions confused me.	These disorganized, vague instructions left me with no idea how to repair the leak.
Toy Story is a good movie with fun for all.	*Toy Story* is a clever animated film with humor, adventure, and romance.
We had a nice time with you.	We enjoyed eating your food, drinking your wine, and swimming in your pool.

Nouns	
I always have trouble with this computer.	I can never get this computer to save or to print.
I like to have fun when I take a vacation.	I like to swim, fish, and eat out when I'm on vacation.
Let me grab some things from my locker.	Let me grab my purse and books from my locker.

ABSTRACT VS. CONCRETE

Abstract language refers to intangible ideas or to classes of people and objects rather than the people or things themselves. Abstractions are built on concrete ideas. Without a grasp of the concrete meanings, a reader can't be expected to understand an abstract idea. Journalists and law enforcement professionals are especially aware of the distinction between abstract and concrete as they write. They strive to present the facts clearly, so the reader can draw conclusions. They avoid making the assumptions for the reader, hoping the facts will speak for themselves. Concrete language requires more time and thought to write, but it communicates a message more effectively. Additional words are an advantage if they add meaning or increase precision.

Abstract Assumption	Concrete Details
Strader was drunk.	Strader smelled strongly of alcohol, slurred his words when he spoke, and stumbled often as he walked.
The couple was in love.	The couple held hands, kissed often, hugged, and ignored everything around them.
Billie is reliable and responsible.	Billie always arrives on time, completes her assignments, and helps others if she has time.

CLICHÉS

A cliché is a tired, overworked phrase that sucks the life out of writing. These are cliché phrases: *a needle in a haystack, quiet as a mouse, crack of dawn, tough as nails, naked truth, hear a pin drop,* and so on. Authors use clichés when they don't have the time or ability to come up with language that is more precise or more meaningful. Although clichés are a sort of "communication shorthand," they rely on stereotypical thinking for their meaning. A writer who uses clichés is relying on unoriginal, worn-out thinking patterns to carry a message. If the message is important, fresh language will make a stronger impression than old, overused phrases. Original language stimulates thought and heightens the reader's concentration. Moreover, a fresh image rewards a reader who is paying close attention to what you have written.

Imagine that a writer wanted to explain how difficult it was to find the source of a problem. Look at the two versions presented below. One relies on a cliché to communicate the message; the other uses a fresher, more original approach. Which version is likely to make the stronger impression, to communicate the message more effectively?

Finding the source of this problem was harder than finding a needle in a haystack.
Finding the source of this problem was harder than finding a fact in a political advertisement.

Here are two more examples contrasting clichés with fresher, more original language. When you check your writing, look for ways to replace frequently used words and phrases with something fresh and original.

We rose at the crack of dawn.
We rose with the roosters.

Having Sam at our negotiations meetings was like having a loose cannon on deck.
Having Sam at our negotiations meetings was like having a German shepherd's tail in your crystal closet.

JARGON

Jargon is the technical, wordy language used by those associated with a trade or profession. Often it is full of passive voice, acronyms, technical terms, and abstract words. Writers use jargon in an attempt to sound educated, sophisticated, or knowledgeable. Actually, jargon muddies and even distorts the message. Compare the following two paragraphs.

Alex demonstrates a tendency to engage inappropriately in verbal social interaction during class time. His grades are deficient because he suffers from an unwillingness to complete supplementary assignments between class periods.

Alex talks in class when he isn't supposed to. He has low grades because he doesn't do his homework.

The first paragraph above leaves the impression that Alex is a sociopath with a serious problem. The second portrays him as a student who needs to talk less and work more. When you write, strive for clear, plain language that communicates your message accurately. Clear communication leaves a better impression by far than pretentious, abstract, jargon-filled words.

PRACTICE

Choose the option that expresses the idea most clearly and concisely. Answers are at the end of the lesson.

5. a. On June 17, Dr. Sam Boswell and Ms. Lorene Webb had an argument over a parking space in the Eagle Supermarket parking lot. Police officers told them both to go home instead of arresting them.
   b. On or about June 17, in the Eagle Supermarket parking lot, Dr. Sam Boswell and Ms. Lorene Webb were allegedly involved in an altercation over a parking space. The police were called. There were no arrests. Both parties were advised to go home by the police officers.

6. a. The most expeditious option in a situation such as this is inevitably also the most advantageous option.

   b. The fastest way is the best way.

7. a. Too many television viewers prefer mindless entertainment to thought-provoking programs.

   b. Too many television viewers prefer "Gilligan's Island" to "The MacNeil-Lehrer Report."

8. a. The research department found that customers are not satisfied with our magazines.

   b. Consumer attitude studies by the research department clearly indicated an extremely low level of customer satisfaction with regard to our newsstand products.

Skill Building Until Next Time

Listen to public officials as they deliver prepared speeches. Do they speak clearly and plainly, or are they trying to sound "official"? A truly competent, intelligent speaker or writer doesn't need a mask of presentious, abstract, sophisticated-sounding language.

ANSWERS

1. Stephanie has contributed a lot to this company's success.

2. Some educators believe that unruly students should be spanked.

3. Using computers can save time and money.

4. I let my supervisor beat me at golf so that she would promote me.

5. a.

6. b.

7. b.

8. a.

MORE DICTION

19

LESSON SUMMARY

This lesson continues the ideas presented in the last lesson: writing clearly and communicating accurately. It covers colloquialism, loaded language, consistent point of view, parallelism, and gender-neutral language.

Good writers know that communicating requires choosing words carefully. Writing styles that are too formal or informal, inappropriate, or just plain emotional, turn readers off. You may have the best ideas in the world, but if you can't get them across in writing, no one will ever act on your great ideas. On the other hand, commonplace ideas that are well expressed are more likely to get attention. How you choose your words has everything to do with whether your writing gets the attention it deserves.

COLLOQUIALISM

Colloquialisms are informal words and phrases such as *a lot, in a bind, pulled it off*, and so on. These words and phrases are widely used in conversations between friends, but in written communication they portray an attitude of chumminess or close friendship that may cause your message to be taken less seriously than you intended. You may even insult your reader without meaning to. A friendly, colloquial tone is fine in a personal letter; however, a more formal tone is better for business communications, which are meant to be taken seriously. Compare the following paragraphs. If you received these two memos from an employee, which would you take more seriously?

I think the way we promote people around here stinks. People who aren't that good at their jobs get promoted just because they pal around with the right people. That puts across the idea that it doesn't matter how much time I put in at work or how good of a job I do; I won't get promoted unless I kiss up to the boss. I'm not that kind of guy.

I think our promotion system is unfair. Average and below average employees receive promotions simply because they befriend their superiors. This practice leaves the impression that commitment and quality of work are not considered. I choose not to socialize with my supervisors, and I feel as though I am not being promoted for that reason alone.

The writer of the first paragraph sounds as if he doesn't take his job all that seriously. And yet he probably does; he just hasn't managed to communicate his seriousness in writing because he has used language that is more appropriate in a conversation with his friends than a memo to his supervisor. The writer of the second paragraph, on the other hand, conveys his seriousness by using more formal language. He has done so without falling into the opposite trap, discussed in the last lesson, of trying to sound *too* intelligent. He has used plain, but not colloquial, language.

The following sentences illustrate the difference between colloquial and formal diction. By substituting the highlighted words, the sentence becomes more formal rather than colloquial.

Colloquial	More Formal Words
I have around three hours to finish this job.	I have **about** three hours to finish this task.
The pasta was real good.	The pasta was **very** good.
We got sick from the food.	We **became ill** from the food.
It looks like we could win.	It looks **as if** we could win.
I'm awful tired.	I'm **very** (or **quite** or **extremely**) tired.

TONE

Tone describes a writer's emotional attitude toward the subject or the audience. The more reasonable and objective a message seems, the more likely it is to be considered seriously. Raging emotions seldom convince anyone to change an opinion, and they seldom convince anyone who is undecided. Persuasion requires clearly presented facts and logically presented arguments. A reader or listener will give the most credibility to an argument that seems fair and objective. Emotion can reduce credibility. Use it carefully.

AVOID ANGER

Avoid accusatory, angry words that make demands. Consider the two paragraphs below. Which one is most likely to persuade the reader to take action?

I just got this stupid credit card bill in the mail. None of these outrageous charges are mine. I can't believe some big corporation like yours can't find a way to keep its records straight or keep its customers from being cheated. If you can't do any better than that, why don't you just give it up? I reported my stolen credit card five days before any of these charges were made, and yet you idiots have charged me for these purchases. The fine print you guys are so fond of putting in all of your contracts says I am not (I'll say it again just to help you understand) **not** responsible for these charges. I want them removed immediately.

The credit card bill I received on April 25 contains several charges that need to be removed. I reported my stolen credit card on April 20. When I called to make the report, the representative referred me the original contract that states, "No charges in excess of $50.00 nor any made more than 24 hours after the card has been reported stolen shall be charged to the customer's account." Naturally, I was quite relieved. All of the charges on this account were made more than 24 hours after I reported the stolen card. Please remove the charges from my account. Thank you very much.

No matter how angry you might be, giving your reader the benefit of the doubt is not only polite but also more likely to get results. (This principle is even more important when you're writing a supervisor, employee, or client than when you're writing a big credit card company.) The first letter is the one you might write in the heat of the moment when you first get your credit card bill. In fact, writing that letter might help you get the anger out of your system. Tearing it up will make you feel even better. *Then* you can sit down and write the letter you're actually going to send—the second version.

Use *sarcasm* (bitter, derisive language) and *irony* (saying the opposite of what you actually mean) carefully in your writing. Like anger, sarcasm brings your credibility into question. Overusing sarcasm can make you seem childish or petty rather than reasonable and logical. Furthermore, in order for irony to be successful, the reader must immediately recognize it. Unless the reader fully understands, you risk confusing or distorting your message. A little well-placed irony or sarcasm may invigorate your writing, but it requires careful, skillful use.

AVOID CUTENESS

Avoid words that make your writing sound flippant, glib, or cute. Although the writing may be entertaining to the reader, it might not be taken seriously. The paragraph below protests a decision, but fails to offer a single reason why the decision was wrong. It may get the attention of the reader, but it won't produce any results, except perhaps the dismissal of its author.

I'm just a li'l ol' girl, but it's clear to me that this decision is dead wrong. I'm afraid that the people who made it have a serious intelligence problem. If they took their two IQ points and rubbed them together, they probably couldn't start gasoline on fire. If you were one of those people…. Oh well, it's been nice working for you.

The conclusion implied in this writer's last sentence—that she doesn't expect to work here much longer—is probably accurate.

AVOID POMPOUSNESS

Avoid words that make your writing sound pompous or preachy. Few people respond positively to a condescending, patronizing tone. Compare the two paragraphs below, both written by employees seeking a promotion. Which employee would you promote if they were both vying for the same position and had nearly identical work records and qualifications?

If you examine my service and work record for the past two years, I believe you will find a dedicated, hardworking employee who is ideal for the floor manager position. I believe all employees should be on time for their jobs. You will see that my attendance record is impeccable, no absences and no tardies. You can see from my monthly evaluations that I was a high-quality employee when I was hired and that I have consistently maintained my high standards. I strive to be the kind of employee all managers wish to hire, and I believe my record shows this. I am also extremely responsible. Again, my record will reflect that my supervisors have confidence in me and assign additional responsibility readily to me because I am someone who can handle it. I am a man of my word, and believe that responsibility is something to be treasured, not shirked. As you compare me with other employees, I feel confident that you will find I am the most competent person available.

Thank you for considering me for the position of floor manager. As you make your decision, I would like to highlight three items from my service and work record. First, in two years I have not missed work and have been tardy only once, as the result of an accident. Second, my supervisors have given me the highest ratings on each of the monthly evaluations. Finally, I was pleased to have been given additional responsibilities during my supervisors' vacation times, and I learned a great deal about managing sales and accounts as a result. I welcome the challenge that would come with a promotion. Thank you again for your consideration.

Both writers highlight the same aspects of their employment records. Yet the first writer seems so full of himself that his superiors might wonder whether he has the people skills to be an effective supervisor. No one wants to work for a supervisor who is prone to such pronouncements as "responsibility is something to be treasured, not shirked." The other writer's just-the-facts approach is bound to make a better impression on the decision-makers.

AVOID CHEAP EMOTION

Avoid language that is full of sentimentality or cheap emotion. You risk making your reader gag. The following paragraph illustrates this error.

We were so deeply hurt by your cruel thoughtlessness in failing to introduce us to Charlton Heston. He is the most wonderful, talented, masculine actor to have ever walked the face of the earth. My friend Charlotte and I so admire him and have ever since we can remember. Our admiration is a deep-channeled river that will never stop flowing. I'm sure you can imagine just how sorely disappointed and deeply wounded we were when we were not given the opportunity and honor to shake the hand and hear the voice of this great man. Neither I nor my dearest friend can seem to forget this slight, and I'm sure we will remain scarred for many years to come.

Are you gagging yet? Instead of regretting not having introduced the writer to the great Charlton Heston, the reader probably congratulates himself on not having let this nut case get near him.

CONSISTENT POINT OF VIEW

Authors can write using the first person point of view (*I, me, we, us, my, our*), second person point of view (*you, your*), or third person point of view (*she, he, one, they, her, him, them, hers, his, one's, theirs*). Avoid switching points of view within or between sentences. Keep the point of view consistent throughout.

Inconsistent	Consistent
Citizens pay taxes, which entitles them [third person] to have some say in how their [third person] government is run. We [first person] have a right to insist on efficient use of our tax dollars.	We citizens pay taxes, which entitles us to have some say in how our government is run. We have a right to insist on efficient use of our tax dollars.
I [first person] enjoyed my trip to the park. You [second person] could see trees budding, flowers blooming, and baby animals running all over.	I enjoyed my trip to the park. I saw trees budding, flowers blooming, and baby animals running all over.

PARALLELISM

Two or more equivalent ideas in a sentence that have the same purpose should be presented in the same form. This is called *parallel structure*. Using parallel sentence structures not only helps your writing flow smoothly, but also helps readers quickly recognize similar ideas. Look at the following examples of parallel words, phrases, and clauses.

Not Parallel	Parallel
My roommate is miserly, sloppy, and a bore.	My roommate is miserly, sloppy, and boring. My roommate is a miser, a slob, and a bore.
My vacuum cleaner squealed loudly, shook violently, and dust filled the air.	My vacuum cleaner squealed loudly, shook violently, and filled the air with dust.
We soon discovered that our plane tickets were invalid, that our cruise reservations had never been made, and our travel agent left town.	We soon discovered that our plane tickets were invalid, that our cruise reservations had never been made, and that our travel agent had left town.

Pairs of ideas should always be presented in parallel constructions. The following sentences present two or more equivalent ideas using similar forms.

> The committee finds no original and inspiring ideas in your proposal. What is original is not inspiring, and what is inspiring is not original.
> We came, we saw, we conquered.
> Belle was a timid, talented, and creative person.
> Ask not what your country can do for you; ask what you can do for your country.

USING GENDER-NEUTRAL LANGUAGE

It may seem that language is neutral, simply a tool for expressing ideas. Although this is partly true, our language reflects our values and communicates to others our social biases about gender and other issues. If an entire culture is gender-biased, the language automatically becomes a vehicle for expressing and perpetuating those biases. One of the first steps toward overcoming such a prejudice is to examine the language and change it so that it no longer perpetuates false stereotypes about gender.

Some people resist changing the language, thinking that the words are harmless and that those who are offended are simply too sensitive. The fact remains that many readers are sensitive to and offended by the traditional use of masculine pronouns to refer to both sexes or by diminutive suffixes indicating gender. Saying, "Man must fulfill his destiny" or "Emily Dickinson was a great poetess" strikes them as archaic at best and insulting at worst.

Whenever emotionally charged words distract a reader, the message suffers. A reader who is offended by the words won't get the meaning.

GENDER TRAPS

Below are samples of the type of language to avoid because the emotional charge may sidetrack the ideas.

Masculine Nouns or Pronouns

The most serious difficulty comes when using pronouns. If the pronoun *he* is used to refer to an indefinite person—a teacher, a student, a postal carrier—the underlying assumption seems to be that all teachers or students or postal carriers are male. The same problem comes up with words such as *someone, somebody, everyone, no one,* or *nobody.* Below are some examples of gender traps in sentences and possible ways to revise them.

Poor	Better
A presidential candidate must realize his life is no longer his own.	Presidential candidates must realize that their that lives are not their own
If a student wishes to change his schedule, he must see his advisor, who will tell him how to proceed.	a) If a student wishes to change his or her schedule, he or she must see his or her advisor, who will tell him how to proceed. [This sentence solves the mismatching number problem by using both a masculine and a feminine singular pronoun. However, the writing seems awkward and unwieldy.] b) If students wish to change their schedule, they must see their advisor, who will tell them how to proceed. [In this sentence, making the noun *student* into plural *students* solves the pronoun mismatch problem.] c) If you wish to change your schedule, see your advisor, who will tell you how to proceed. [This sentence uses the 2nd person pronouns "you" and "your."]
If anyone wants to improve his test scores, he should take good notes and study.	a) Anyone who wants improved test scores should take good notes and study. [Restructure the sentence to avoid the pronoun reference.] b) Students who want to improve their test scores should take good notes and study. [Turn *anyone* into the plural *students.*] c) Anyone who wants to improve his or her test scores should take good notes and study. [Use both the masculine and feminine singular pronouns.]

Note that you cannot simply change the words *he* and *his* to *they* and *theirs*. "If anyone wants to improve their test scores, they should good take notes and study" is grammatically incorrect. The pronouns *they* and *their* don't match their antecedent, anyone, in number, because *anyone* is singular and *they* is plural.

Women as Subordinate to Men

There are many subtle ways in which writers can make it seem as if men are always leaders and women are always subordinate.

Poor	Better
A principal and his staff need to establish good communication.	The principal and staff need to establish good communication.
If you ask the nurse, she will summon the doctor if he is available.	If you ask, a nurse will summon an available doctor.
Bob took his wife and children to a movie.	Bob and Mary took their children to a movie.
Emil asked his secretary to check the mail.	Emil asked the secretary to check the mail.

Writers also fall into a similar kind of trap when they refer to men according to their abilities, while referring to women according to their appearance.

Poor	Better
Dr. Routmeir and his attractive, blond wife arrived at the party at 9:00 P.M.	a) Dr. and Ms. Routmeir arrived at the party at 9:00 P.M. b) Herman and Betty Routmeir arrived at the party at 9:00 P.M.
The talented violinist and his beautiful accompanist took the stage.	The violinist and the accompanist took the stage.

Note that in both sentences in the first column above, the man is referred to by his profession, while the woman is referred to by her appearance. To avoid the appearance of assigning value to men because of their accomplishments and to women because of their appearance, refer to both in the same context, either physical or professional. Furthermore, in the first example the man is addressed by a formal title, and the woman is not identified except as the wife belonging to the man. To avoid the appearance of referring to the woman strictly as the possession of the man, refer to both by name.

"Men's" Jobs and "Women's" Jobs

Avoid making special note of gender when discussing a job traditionally done by men or women—those traditions don't hold any more! The first sentence below makes traditional assumptions, while the second does not.

> When a man on board collapsed, a lady pilot emerged from the cockpit, and a male nurse offered assistance.
>
> When a passenger collapsed, a pilot emerged from the cockpit, and a nurse offered assistance.

The references *lady pilot* and *male nurse* call attention to themselves because they assume that the reader will automatically assign a gender to the job. Readers who do not think in terms of the traditional stereotypes will be offended by the writer's assumption that they do engage in stereotypical thinking.

AVOIDING GENDER TRAPS

As a writer, you must understand the effect of gender references on readers. You can avoid offending readers unintentionally with gender-specific language in three ways: using gender-neutral terms, using the plural, or restructuring sentences altogether to avoid a gender reference. All of these tactics have already been illustrated in the revised sentences above. More examples appear below.

Use Gender-Neutral Terms

There are a lot of words in English that traditionally have taken different forms for male and female persons. These distinctions are becoming obsolete. Nowadays, most people prefer one term to refer to both men and women in their particular roles. And this change doesn't have to be awkward, as you can see in the table below.

Gender-Specific	Gender-Neutral
waiter, waitress	server
stewardess, steward	flight attendant
policeman, policewoman	police officer
chairwoman, chairman	chairperson, chair
man-made	synthetic, artificial
foreman	supervisor
manpower	employees, personnel
man, mankind	humanity, people

In the past, it was common to use the word man to refer to all humanity, both men and women. Nowadays, that usage will offend many readers. The sentence below demonstrates this kind of usage while the second one offers a more appropriate alternative.

> If man wishes to improve his environment, he must improve himself.
>
> If Humanity wishes to improve its environment, each individual must improve.

Convert to the Plural

One of the stickiest gender-reference problems is how to deal with a sentence such as, "A student must do *his* homework if *he* wants to succeed in *his* classes." The easiest way to avoid those troublesome *he* words is to turn the singular pronouns *he, she, him, hers,* or *his* into the plural pronouns *they* and *their.* Of course, then you must also revise the antecedents of those pronouns so they are also plural. (See Lesson 13): "*Students* must do *their* homework if *they* want to succeed in *their* classes." Here are some other examples.

Gender-Specific	Gender-Neutral
The doctor uses his best judgment.	Doctors use their best judgment.
Every student must do his homework.	Students must do their homework.
A company executive is wise to choose his words carefully.	Company executives are wise to choose their words carefully.
If a professor wants respect, he should behave respectably.	Professors who want respect should behave respectably.

Restructure Sentences to Avoid Gender Reference

Finally, you can avoid gender references altogether by restructuring your sentences. See how this is done in the following examples.

Gender-Specific	Gender-Neutral
Man has always turned to his intellect to solve problems.	People have always turned to their intellect to solve problems.
A company executive is wise to drive himself relentlessly.	Anyone who desires success must work relentlessly.
A nurse must take her job seriously.	A nurse must take the job seriously.
Someone left his umbrella in the cloakroom. He should call Lost and Found.	The person who left an umbrella in the cloakroom should call Lost and Found.
The ladies enjoyed the shopping trip.	The shoppers enjoyed their trip.

Skill Building Until Next Time

Pay close attention to the tone and style of everything you write or read. Is the degree of formality appropriate for the message and the audience? Do you sense emotional overload? Is the point of view consistent? Are equivalent ideas presented equally? Does the writing contain gender references? If so, are they likely to offend the reader?

L·E·S·S·O·N 20

COMMUNICATING YOUR IDEAS

LESSON SUMMARY

The previous lessons have dealt with words and sentences. This final lesson is about the bigger issues involved in a piece of writing as a whole. By focusing on the purpose of your writing, you can develop your ideas in a logical, effective way to have the biggest possible impact on your readers.

Mastering writing detail is important, but the main purpose of writing is to communicate a message with a specific purpose to an audience. Most writing does one of three things: inform, explain, or present an argument. Writing effectively involves discovering what you want to say, organizing your ideas, and presenting them in the most logical, effective way. This lesson discusses all of these issues.

WRITING TO INFORM

Good, informational writing is clear, simple, and orderly. In all business writing and in most of the writing you'll do in college, it's important to get right to the point. No one has time to spend reading your warm-ups, the words you write while you're trying to get to the point. The best communications state the point directly and present the information clearly.

However, sometimes getting started is difficult. Asking yourself a few key questions will help you clarify your thoughts and get to the point.

1. Summarize the main idea of your communication in a single sentence. If you can do this, the rest of the writing will come more easily. State it as simply and clearly as possible. If your communication presents a list of information, facts, or statistics, try summarizing the purpose of the information. The sentence should answer the question: Why am I writing this?

2. Next, think about your audience. Who will be reading your writing? What is your relationship with the audience: professor, superior, colleague, customer? Thinking about the audience helps you to use an appropriate tone or attitude.

3. Brainstorm all the information that must be included in the communication. This can be in the form of a list or a piece of paper with words and pictures connected by lines; use whatever works best for you. Get all the information down on paper where you can look at it.

4. Once the information is all assembled, think about the most efficient way to organize it. Think about your message as a train of thought, one in which all the parts are connected. How can you organize the information in such a way that connections seem easy and natural? Consider these organizational patterns:

   - **Spatial order:** the order in which items are arranged in relationship to each other
   - **Chronological order:** time order
   - **Logical order:** begin with the most basic premise, follow with what can be derived from the premise
   - **General to specific:** begin with a general statement, arrive at a specific fact
   - **Specific to general:** arrive at a generalization from a series of specific facts

5. Now it's time to start writing. Begin with a sentence or short paragraph that states the purpose of the communication, revising what you came up with in Step 1 now that you know what your main points are.

6. Develop each of the ideas you identified in Steps 3 and 4 in a single paragraph. If the supporting ideas can be presented as effectively in list form as they can in sentence form, use a bulleted list similar to the one above that outlines organizational patterns. Stick to one idea in each paragraph and keep the paragraphs as short and concise as possible.

If you're writing for business use numbered and bulleted lists like the ones on this page. If it's college writing, you can work with longer paragraphs—just make sure you follow the rules for using evidence in the discipline you're writing for (see Lesson 21). Strive for a clear, logical presentation, one that is well organized and free of excess words that say nothing. Here's a map of one writer's organizational process in responding to a request: the planning, the organization, the main idea, the audience, and the completed memo.

The Planning

Allie McGinnis has a work-study job in the sociology department. The department chairperson asked her to compile information about the printers used in the department and draft a memo to the technology coordinator for the department.

Main idea: Mr. Lundsky requested information about the printers (models, date of purchase) used in the sociology department and justification for the technology requests they made last year.

Purpose: Provide the information so the department can get what it requested.

Audience: Mr. Lundsky, technology coordinator

I. Data
    A. Current computers and memory
        1. PS1, 4 mb RAM
        2. PS2, 8 mb RAM
        3. AST, 8 mb RAM
        4. PS2, 8 mb RAM
        5. Compaq Presario, 16 mb RAM
    B. Printers
        1. NEC, 1991
        2. Epson, 1992
        3. HP Laserjet II, 1993
        4. HP Deskjet 560, 1995

II. Requests
    A. Additional printer
        1. HP Deskjet 660C for Compaq Presario
        2. Reason: newest, most powerful computer needs color capability
    B. Memory upgrades
        1. two 8 mb SIMMs for PS1
        2. two 8 mb SIMMs for PS2s respectively
        3. 8 mb SIMMs for AST
    C. Justification for memory upgrades
        1. Most recent programs require a minimum of 16 mb RAM
        2. 8 mb SIMMs are the most cost effective

The Memo

To: Mr. Lundsky

From: Allie McGinnis

Re: Technology assessment and needs of sociology department as requested

Date: May 9, 1996

I am providing the information you requested about equipment we have in our department. I am also outlining our additional requests and the reasons for these requests.

These are the machines, memory capacity, and printers we have at this time:

- PS1, 4 mb RAM, NEC Silentwriter printer (purchased in 1991)
- PS2, 8 mb RAM, Epson LQ2 dot matrix printer (both purchased in 1992)
- AST, 8 mb RAM, no printer (purchased in 1992)
- PS2, 8 mb RAM, Laserjet II printer (both purchased in 1993)
- Compaq Presario, 16 mb RAM, HP Deskjet 560 (purchased 1995)

We are requesting five 8-megabyte memory SIMMs to upgrade all of the computers to at least 16 mb of RAM. The most recent programs we have purchased require a minimum of 10 mb. Eight-mb SIMMS are the most cost-effective way to buy additional memory. A single 8-mb SIMMs is $95.00, while 4-mb SIMMs are $72.00 and 2-mb SIMMs are $59.00 each. We also need an HP Deskjet 660C. We plan to move the HP Deskjet 560 to the AST, which has no printer, and put the new printer with color capability on our newest, most powerful unit.

Thank you for considering our request.

WRITING TO EXPLAIN

Another form of writing you're likely to use often is explanation. In the "real world," you may need to provide reasons for an action or policy, or you may need to explain how a product is used. In college, you may have to explain a historical event or the process you used in a scientific experiment.

For this type of writing, follow the same planning process as you would for a written communication designed to present information.

1. Summarize the main idea and purpose.

2. Determine the audience.

3. Brainstorm ideas.

4. Organize the ideas.

5. Begin by stating the purpose.

6. Develop the ideas in paragraphs.

Keep these tips in mind as you write.

- Present the steps in a logical order. Chronological order is usually best for a process.
- Be certain you've explained each step clearly, accurately, and thoroughly enough for a reader to be able to understand.
- Use the facts garnered from your reading and research to support each of your points. See Lesson 22 for advice on how to cite the sources of your research.
- Pay special attention to the introduction and conclusion. These two paragraphs lay the foundation for understanding and give the reader a quick review of the information you've just presented. Make the beginning and ending paragraphs work for you.

Here's a real-world example: the planning one writer did before drafting a letter to a customer explaining how to operate a new copy machine.

Main idea: explain to new customer how to use a new copy machine
Audience: members of promotional staff at KCBD-TV, all of whom use the copier
Purposes: (1) clearly explain use, (2) clearly outline maintenance procedures, (3) provide basic trouble-shooting suggestions, (4) assure them that the copier is reliable and that service is quick, should they need it.

   I. Daily use
      A. Copying
      B. Enlarging/reducing
      C. Handling multiple-page documents
  II. Maintenance
      A. Routine
         1. Loading paper
         2. Adding toner
         3. Clearing paper jams
      B. Troubleshooting
         1. Electrical problems
         2. Paper jams
         3. Failure to copy
      C. Calling the technician
         1. Business day number
         2. Emergency service

III. Reliability
   A. Warranties
   B. Weekly maintenance checks
   C. Service
   D. Two-hour replacement guarantee

First paragraph: Everyone in the promotional department at KCBD-TV will find this new Sharp copy machine a huge improvement over the older model. You'll appreciate how easy it is to use this new copier for daily tasks, and anyone can perform the routine maintenance on the machine. This, our most reliable copier, is backed by a long-term warranty and a quick, efficient service plan.

WRITING TO PERSUADE

The other most common type of writing involves presenting a clear, convincing argument. Your written communication may be a single message, or it may be the first in a series of exchanges that will eventually result in a compromise. Each type of argument requires a different approach; however, both kinds of persuasive communications must have three common characteristics: logical order, solid support, and credibility.

LOGICAL ORDER

Even the brightest and best ideas make no impact if a reader cannot recognize or follow them. Arguments must be carefully organized to create the desired effect on the reader.

The strongest positions are the beginning and the ending of a communication. Place your strongest argument in one position or the other and arrange the rest in such a way that they can be clearly stated and easily linked together.

SOLID SUPPORT

Good persuasion not only makes a clear, strong claim but also proves the claim with solid support. Here are some ways to support your assertions:

- **Examples,** either personal or researched.
- **Objective evidence,** such as facts and statistics.
- **Citing an authority.** Use a qualified, timely authority whose opinions are applicable to your special situations. If the reader is not familiar with the authority, explain why the person is qualified.
- **Analogy.** If you can think of a clear comparison with which the reader is automatically familiar, present the comparison clearly. Carefully point out all of the similarities and explain why the comparison is useful and applicable.

If you are supporting a moral or emotional claim, use logic or emotional appeals made with vivid description and concrete language.

CREDIBILITY

A written communication is *credible* if the reader believes the writer or finds the writer trustworthy. Regardless of the history between the writer and reader, each communication provides a fresh opportunity to establish credibility.

In any communication, you can establish credibility in one of three ways:

- **Demonstrate your knowledge of the subject.** Show that you have personal experience that makes your perspective on the subject reliable. If, as in most academic writing, you have no personal experience from which to draw, show that you have consulted a variety of reliable, neutral sources and that your views are based on your research.
- **Demonstrate fairness and objectivity.** Show that you have taken into account all of the significant viewpoints. Convince your reader that you understand and value other perspectives on the subject and that you see their merit. Show that you have carefully considered all of the evidence, even that which does not support your point of view.
- **Seek areas of agreement.** This is especially valuable if your communication is the beginning of a process that will result in a compromise. Find out what the viewpoints have in common and begin building trust and credibility on common ground.

Use the same six steps outlined above to plan a persuasive communication. Examine the following writer's plan for a written communication that argues in favor of a new scheduling policy.

Claim: store needs a better system for scheduling employees

Audience: store's general manager

Purposes: (1) point out problems inherent in the current policy, (2) outline the qualities a new scheduling policy should have, (3) point out the advantages of a scheduling policy with those qualities, (4) show that customers will receive better service, (5) show that employees understand and are willing to share the burden of developing and implementing a new policy.

I. Problems with current policy
   A. Based solely upon seniority
   B. Arbitrary within seniority brackets
   C. Equal number for all shifts
      1. Doesn't allow for employees willing to be flexible
      2. Not enough employees during peak sales times
      3. Too many employees during off-peak sales times
      4. Leads to minimal employee commitment
   D. No incentive for good attendance

II. Qualities of an effective scheduling policy
   A. Continues to take seniority into account
   B. Allows for individual preferences
   C. Allows for flex time
   D. Allows for increased numbers during peak times, reduced numbers during off times
   E. Provides an incentive for reliable attendance
   F. Provides an incentive to work least desirable hours
III. Advantages of a policy with these characteristics
   A. Improved customer service
      1. Better service during peak times
      2. Quality service during off-peak times
   B. Less absenteeism
   C. Improved employee morale
   D. Sense of ownership among employees
IV. Development and implementation
   A. Management responsibilities
   B. Employee responsibilities
      1. Committee willing to develop plan during unpaid time
      2. Willing to assume some responsibility for implementation

First paragraph: Since we value customer service, our store needs to develop a scheduling system that will provide better customer service while at the same time fostering an increased sense of commitment among employees.

Whenever you write, keep in mind that you want to present your message as clearly and simply as possible. Write to **express**, not to **impress**. The words should deliver the message, not get in the way of it.

Skill Building Until Next Time

Use the six-step planning process outlined in this lesson on your next paper for one of your courses. If you don't have to write any papers this term, try something really tough: a persuasive memo or letter that convinces someone in authority to do something he or she may not want to do. Write your boss a memo asking for a raise. Write your instructor a letter explaining why a final exam is not necessary in this course. Convince the academic dean that most classes should meet twice a week rather than three times. Whatever your write, be sure to use the six-step planning process.

WRITING ACROSS THE COLLEGE CURRICULUM

21

LESSON SUMMARY

This chapter addresses the issue of writing in the different disciplines your studies encompass. You'll learn strategies for becoming a competent writer regardless of the discipline. You'll also learn about basic organizational patterns and the types of writing you'll encounter in the humanities, social sciences, and natural sciences.

As a beginning college student, you may be surprised to find you have to learn different ways of writing for different courses you take. There are different "rules," commonly called *conventions*, for writing in an English course than for a biology course or a history course. Some conventions, of course, apply to writing in any course you take. All of your instructors will expect to see correctly written sentences with all the words spelled correctly and all the punctuation in the right places. In addition, all college writing should be organized according to some clearly discernible pattern. But the *kinds* of writing you'll do in various classes will be different from each other; there are some patterns that are more common in the sciences, for instance, than in the humanities, while patterns that are common in the humanities are not necessarily used in the social sciences.

This lesson will show you the most common patterns used in three broad categories of college classes: humanities, social sciences, and natural sciences. First, however, you'll learn what you should pay attention to in order to learn to write well for a particular discipline.

How to Learn to Write for a Particular Discipline

Writing in any discipline requires careful thinking and organization. The formats and organizational patterns differ greatly from discipline to discipline, even from instructor to instructor, but several basic principles apply in all cases. Understanding them and following them is the first step toward writing competently.

LEARN THE VOCABULARY

Every discipline has its own terminology or jargon. Learn it! Once you understand the words, you can begin using them as you think, talk, and write.

READ! READ! READ!

Few things improve writing as much as reading. By immersing yourself in the content, you begin to internalize the vocabulary, concepts, and organizational patterns characteristic of the discipline. Do your assigned reading. It will help your test scores, but it will also improve your writing. Read supplementary assignments and scholarly journals in the disciplines you study. Honestly, few things improve your writing as much as careful, active reading. As you read, you'll subconsciously adopt the tone and style of the writing. Consciously note other things, such as sentence length and complexity, point of view, bibliography styles, and visual representations of information. Whenever you write, use what you've learned from your reading.

EXAMINE THE EVIDENCE

Much of what you read will be evidence in support of an argument, an idea, or a point of view. Pay careful attention to what kind of evidence is used. Think about these categories and questions.

- **Statistics.** How often are statistics used? To what extent are they used? What kinds of statistics do you find in your reading?
- **Empirical data.** What kind of objective, measurable data is used in support of arguments?
- **Research.** What kind of research do you see in your reading? Is it mostly primary research (the kind that goes directly to the source, such as interviews, letters, etc.) or is it mostly secondary research (reviews of current literature, examining and interpreting the findings of others)? To what degree are quotations used? How are they used?
- **Authority.** Who are the recognized authorities in the field? What does it take to be recognized as an authority? How do they establish their credibility?
- **Reasoning.** What kind of logic supports an argument? How often do writers use definitions or explain cause/effect relationships? Do they use analogies or anecdotes? What kinds of examples are used to make a point?

There you have it! Know the words. Read the words. Analyze the words. Mastering these principles will put you at the head of the pack in your discipline.

WRITING IN THE HUMANITIES

WHAT ARE THE HUMANITIES?

Humanities are those disciplines that help us understand, interpret, and express our humanity—the arts. These include languages, literature, drama, music, dance, drawing, painting, sculpting, film, etc.

HOW TO PREPARE TO WRITE IN THE HUMANITIES

First of all, become familiar with literary terms, such as *figurative language* and *imagery*, those that take the ordinary and mundane to a new level where it is a representation or interpretation of ordinary reality. Although these seem like terms that apply mainly to literature, other humanities use them as well. Many of the concepts in other disciplines correspond with those in literature. Interpretation is the essence of the humanities. Learn the terminology or features of whatever disciplines you study. Practice using the terms when you think about or discuss a piece of work until you become proficient at using them. Address those features or qualities in your writing.

KINDS OF WRITING IN THE HUMANITIES

At least half of the writing you do in an educational setting will be in the humanities. Most writing assignments fall into one of the categories listed below.

Reflective Writing

Reflective writing includes assignments that ask you to reveal and explain your personal response to a work and then use that response to arrive at a personal interpretation. A reflective writing exercise might ask you to make a connection to something in your life or to concentrate on an emotional response you had to a work. For example, you might be asked to identify with a character or an event in a work of literature you have read. Reflective writing also includes assignments that ask for your thoughts about the purpose or theme.

Criticism

A *critique* of a work examines its strengths and weakness for the purposes of making a judgment. It may also evaluate the clearness, accuracy, or value of a piece of work or a system. A critique is based on your individual reactions and interpretations but takes them a step further.

Begin a critical essay by developing a *thesis* around the purpose or theme of a work, making a judgment about how effectively the work accomplishes its purpose. A thesis is a precisely written sentence that states the purpose of an essay in specific terms and suggests how the essay will be developed. Write an essay in support of your thesis by making observations about the features of the work. The thesis is the key to good critical writing. In fact, most kinds of writing in the humanities need a thesis statement. Be careful of thesis statements that are too broad or fail to identify a specific topic.

The critical essay develops and proves the thesis statement, using specific examples for the piece of work. Develop the ideas in paragraphs, each of which deals with a single idea. Organize the paragraphs in a way that makes sense and tie them together with strong transitions. Draw all of your ideas together in the conclusion. Finally, spend time revising the essay and developing an introduction that catches the reader's attention and states the thesis.

THESIS STATEMENTS

Too Broad	Better
The classic George Lucas movie *Return of the Jedi* is a good sequel to *Star Wars*.	The classic George Lucas movie *Return of the Jedi* builds on the plot, characters, and themes introduced in *Star Wars*.
Homer's *Iliad* is a high adventure war story.	Homer's *Iliad* combines heroes, challenges, and action into a classic war story format that is the prototype for modern war epics.

Analysis

Analytical writing asks you to take a close look at the parts of something to see how they operate together to create the whole. In literature, for example, this may mean a close textual analysis of a poem or a section of a story. In other areas, you might be asked to classify or to break down the topic and discuss its parts. You might be asked to compare (find similarities) and contrast (find differences) or to discuss causes and effects. All of these tasks require analysis. In analytical writing, as in critical writing, you should write a strong thesis and then support it in an organized way.

Contextual Writing

Contextual writing asks you to examine the environment (social, intellectual, historical, and economic) in which the subject exists and to discuss the effect of the environment on the subject. Here, too, a strong thesis is important. Support for your thesis will come not only from the work(s) you are discussing but also from the secondary sources that discuss the environment the work comes from.

Creative Writing

Creative assignments ask you to create your own poetry or fiction using your own ideas. If your instructor wants a particular kind of creative writing, he or she will give you directions on how to create it.

Research Writing

A *research* assignment asks you to research a topic thoroughly for the purpose of developing your own ideas about the topic. Even though most of what's in your paper comes from secondary research sources, you still should have *your own thesis,* even if you're simply agreeing with one of the authors you read. Research writing needs to be as carefully organized, developed, and supported as any other kind of writing. A research paper could include criticism, analysis, or contextualization as part of its focus.

Lesson 22, "Documentation," outlines the basics of citing sources in a research paper. Research in the humanities usually follows the MLA format.

WRITING IN THE SOCIAL SCIENCES

WHAT ARE THE SOCIAL SCIENCES?

The social sciences include those disciplines that study human interaction, systems, and societies. History, geography, anthropology, psychology, and sociology are some of the disciplines in the social sciences.

HOW TO PREPARE TO WRITE IN THE SOCIAL SCIENCES

As usual, the best way to learn to write in the social sciences is to read in the social sciences. Pay attention to the vocabulary used and to what counts as evidence.

Writing in the social sciences is scientific, yet personal, since it's about people. Much of the writing follows the problem-solution organizational pattern.

1. **Introduction:** presents the subject and the thesis or problem, previews the development of the essay.

2. **Exposition:** includes background information a reader will need to understand the problem, the observations, the discussion, and the recommendations to come.

3. **Data review:** summarizes current findings and literature on the topic.

4. **New information:** discusses new findings or possible solutions to the problem and their relative merit.

5. **Conclusions and/or recommendations:** presents your thinking about the significance of the topic or your ideas about what should be done.

KINDS OF WRITING IN THE SOCIAL SCIENCES

The most common kinds of writing in the social sciences are listed below.

Case Studies

A *case study* involves research, observation, and reporting. For example, a case study of a family for your sociology class might involve doing background research on the family, recording your own observations over a period of time, and then drawing conclusions based on the research and the new data you have collected.

Position Papers

A *position paper* is actually a pro/con paper, one that presents balanced arguments on both sides of a controversial issue and then draws a conclusion or takes a stand. Usually, a position paper presents background information first, explaining the issue, offering a brief history, and laying the foundation for the arguments. Next, the opposing sides are presented, making certain that each side receives equal treatment, drawing minor conclusions along the way. In the last part of the paper, the analysis, the author draws final conclusions about the issue and suggests a solution or a course of action.

Report on Data Collection

Some instructors in courses such as psychology or sociology will ask you to do your own *primary research*: gathering and analyzing data on a specific task. For instance, you might construct a survey on dating and then ask 50 first-year students and 50 seniors to fill out your survey to see whether there are differences in the way younger and older students approach dating. If you get an assignment like this, your instructor will give you the form you should use to write up your findings; it will be similar to the problem-solution format outlined above.

Research Writing

Writing based on secondary sources may combine aspects of any of the above forms, or your assignment may simply ask you to explain a topic based on several different sources. You still need to develop your own ideas about the topic in order to have a thesis. Be sure to consult the lesson on "Documentation" to help you get started. Research in the social sciences usually follows the APA format.

WRITING IN THE NATURAL SCIENCES

WHAT ARE THE NATURAL SCIENCES?

The natural sciences include biology, chemistry, physics, astronomy, geology, meteorology, oceanography, and other disciplines that deal with the intricate workings of organisms and systems in the natural world.

HOW TO PREPARE TO WRITE IN THE NATURAL SCIENCES

Writing in the natural sciences is highly organized and often accompanied by visual representations of data. As you will see by reading your textbooks and other natural science materials, formats can vary, but one thing that stands out is the importance of *factual* information. There is usually less interpretation involved in writing for the natural sciences than for the social sciences or humanities.

Scientific writing is often organized in a way that corresponds with the scientific method.

1. Identify the problem.

2. Make observations.

3. Form a hypothesis.

4. Gather data.

5. Test the hypothesis.

6. Draw conclusions.

KINDS OF WRITING IN THE NATURAL SCIENCES

The most common kinds of writing in the natural sciences include data collection and reporting, lab reports, and research writing.

Data Collection and Reporting

Writing based on *data collection* requires you to make observations, collect data from those observations, and report the data. Begin by explaining the purpose of the data collection. Go on to describe the methods of observation and the results of the observations. Usually, tables, graphs, and charts are used to report the information. In the final portion of a data report, discuss the results and present your conclusions.

Lab Report

Lab reports are probably the most common type of writing in the natural sciences. This form is used to explain the foundations of an experiment and to report the results. Here is the standard lab report format.

1. **Introduction.** Explain the principles used for the experiment, the problem upon which the experiment is based, and the hypothesis to be tested during the experiment.

2. **Methods/Materials.** Briefly explain the experiment. Include a full discussion of the materials you use and the procedures you follow. This portion of the lab report is what makes it possible for others to duplicate your experiment, so accuracy is vital.

3. **Results.** Tell what happened during the course of the experiment.

4. **Discussion.** This is usually the longest portion of the lab report. It includes commentary about the hypothesis, the methods, and the results. It sets up the final section of a lab report.

5. **Summary/Conclusions.** Since many scientists read this part of the report first and may not even read the rest of the paper, this section includes a brief summary of the experiment before presenting and explaining the significant results or conclusions.

Research Writing

The kinds of writing outlined above involve one kind of research, in which you collect data yourself for the purpose of analyzing it. You may also do *secondary research* for assignments like these in order to see what other scholars have discovered when doing similar experiments. Or you may be asked simply to do secondary research, reading what others have written about a given topic and reporting on it. Even though almost all the ideas in your paper come from someone else, you still are in charge of imposing some kind of order in what you write. A thesis or main idea will help in this process. The lesson on "Documentation" will show you when you need to give credit for others' ideas and how to do it. Pay careful attention to the directions your instructor gives you when you prepare scientific research.

Skill Building Until Next Time

Choose the course you're taking right now that you believe will require the most writing. Try outlining the next two reading assignments you receive in that subject. The outline will help you to understand the format and organizational pattern of the writing for that subject. Use what you learn in the next writing assignment for that subject.

L·E·S·S·O·N

DOCUMENTATION

22

LESSON SUMMARY

This lesson explains how to cite or document sources in a researched essay. You'll learn what needs to be cited and what need not be cited. You'll learn about citing sources within the text of your essay using the MLA and the APA styles of documentation. You'll also learn about the more traditional notes-and-bibliography (also known as Turabian) format.

Many students break into a cold sweat when they hear about documenting information in a research paper. They've heard horror stories from their high school English teachers about the dire consequences of plagiarism—expulsion, incarceration, decapitation, and such. You need not be one of those sweaty students. By learning a few basic principles about documentation, you can write a researched essay that shows competence and original thought. This chapter covers what to document, how to avoid plagiarizing, and how to insure that you document correctly.

WHAT IS RESEARCH?

Research is the process of investigating a topic thoroughly to learn as much as you can about it. As a researcher, you use that information to form your own thoughts and conclusions about the subject. A researched essay reveals and explains your original thinking.

WHAT IS DOCUMENTATION?

Documentation is the act of using notes or citations to give credit to the original sources of opinions, ideas, facts, and statistics used in your research writing.

Why bother to document? Probably the most obvious answer is this: If you don't document properly, you risk failing the research assignment. However, there are a number of very good reasons for doing a competent job of citing your sources.

First of all, good documentation serves as an aid to readers who want to learn more about the subject by consulting your sources. Imagine your are reading a researched essay about digital imaging over phone lines. Let's go on to say that you want to know more about it. If the essay has been properly documented, all you need to do is look at the sources listed at the end of the paper. Without proper documentation, you would need to redo the investigation of the original researcher.

Additionally, proper documentation gives the author credibility. Failure to document or doing a sloppy job calls your integrity as a researcher into question. At best, readers may think you are a careless writer; at worst, they may think you are dishonest. On the other hand, proper documentation makes your research easy to validate. Research is valuable only to the extent that it is reliable, accurate, and objective. Careful attention to detail makes it easy for a reader to assess the validity of your research.

Finally, careful documentation gives credit where credit is due and eliminates any possibility that you may be accused of plagiarism.

WHAT NEED NOT BE DOCUMENTED

Some kinds of information need not be documented, or noted. Two examples are common knowledge and your own opinions.

Common Knowledge

Common knowledge includes any fact or information that could be readily found in more than one reference book. You don't have to cite a source for such information.

```
The stock market fell a record 257 points on August 15, 1997.
These are the procedures for filing a suit in small claims court.
Lumber is an economic mainstay for Minnesota.
```

Your Own Opinions

Ideas and opinions you arrived at on your own need not be documented.

> If secret servicemen had insisted on safety first, President Kennedy would not have been shot during the parade at Dallas.
>
> European settlers eventually treated the North American natives as though they were conquered people who were in some way inferior to them.
>
> Homer's Odyssey is really nothing more than another "Honey, I'm going to be late for dinner" story.

WHAT MUST BE DOCUMENTED

On the other hand, most kinds of information that are not your own ideas must always be documented.

Direct Quotations

Any words directly quoted from a source must be surrounded with quotation marks and noted. This applies even if the quotation is as short as three or four words. Good writers work the source of information into the text of the paper, giving credit within the text as well as with the note. In that case, only the page number (in MLA style) or the date (in ADA style) appears in the parenthetical note.

> Dr. John Mitchell, who has studied witches for decades, writes, "Little is known about the inner workings of most covens" (45).

Paraphrases of Quotations

Quotations taken from a source, even if they are paraphrased, need to be documented with a note.

> Dr. John Mitchell, who has studied witches for decades, reports that details of coven operations are mostly a mystery (45).

Opinions of Others

Any opinion that is not your own must be documented—even if you agree with the opinion.

> According to Jefson, if Pythagoras had lived even thirty years earlier, geometry would have taken many more centuries to develop (32).

Ideas of Others

As with opinions, any ideas that are not your own must be documented.

> One way of solving the waste disposal problem in our city would be to encourage recycling businesses such as Green Thumb to relocate near the landfill (Hartung 10).

Little-Known Facts

As you already know, readily available facts need not be documented. However, facts that are difficult to locate are documented as a service to the reader. A note makes it easy for the reader to verify the fact.

Statistics

Undoubtedly, you've heard that the same statistic can be used to prove two completely opposite arguments. Whenever readers wish to validate research, they usually begin with the statistics cited in the paper. They look to see that the statistics have been accurately represented.

Charts, Graphs, and Any Visual Representation of Data

Much common-knowledge information, such as population data, appears in the form of charts, graphs, or tables. If you use a chart or any visual representation of data in the form in which you found it, you must document it even though it is common knowledge. The documentation gives credit to whoever prepared the data representation.

Questionable Assumptions

Any assumption that might be readily challenged or argued and is not your own should be documented.

```
Martin Luther King's death was the result of a conspiracy (Harden 75).
Greed and a need for power drove Magellan (Fredricks 108).
Shakespeare wrote few of the plays for which he is credited (Dean 210).
```

WHAT IS PLAGIARISM?

Plagiarism is using the work or thinking of someone else and passing it off as your own. It's a type of intellectual theft, which is why plagiarism is frowned on in academic environments.

Few people who plagiarize set out to do so. More often than not, they begin with good intentions, yet end up with a plagiarized paper because of careless research habits. In fact, they may not even realize that their work is plagiarized. Here are some examples of plagiarism that you may not have known were wrong:

- Using the exact words of an original without quotation marks or documentation is always plagiarism. Sometimes this happens because of carelessness, forgetting the quotation marks or the source on a note card. The result is still plagiarism.
- Using the exact words of an original without quotation marks is also plagiarism *even if you document the source*. Quotation marks must enclose any words that are not your own. Telling where you found them is not enough.
- Using someone else's idea in a research paper without citing the source is plagiarism even if the ideas are paraphrased. You must credit the original source.

- Changing a word here and there in a source passage is not paraphrasing and does not make your writing original. Even if you credit the source, you have engaged in something called *patchwork plagiarism*—using most of the original writer's words and sentence structures as if they were your own. Patchwork plagiarism occurs when a writer begins to paraphrase a source but does it poorly.

HOW TO AVOID PLAGIARISM

There are three steps to avoiding plagiarism *as you are doing your research*. You need to take these steps while you are in the library rather than waiting until you sit down to write.

Careful Notes

The first thing to do in trying to avoid plagiarism is to take careful notes. If you aren't sure whether a piece of information needs to be documented, note it. When in doubt, document. You may get to the end of a research paper and realize that virtually every word in the paper is documented. If that happens, you haven't done enough thinking about the topic to have ideas of your own. Take the time to do some thinking!

Summaries

Another way to avoid plagiarism is to summarize as you take notes. When you finish reading a paragraph, stop to think about it, and write what it said in a sentence of your own. A good summary is usually about one-fourth as long as the original passage. Summarizing without looking at the text can eliminate the possibility of plagiarism.

Paraphrases

Yet another way is to paraphrase carefully as you take notes. Paraphrasing is restating what you have read in your own words. Unlike a summary, a paraphrase is usually as long as the original. It simply restates the ideas in your own words, rather than someone else's. Be sure to document, even when summarizing or paraphrasing, if the idea is not your own.

HOW TO DOCUMENT

Whenever you are assigned to do research writing, listen to or read carefully whatever directions your instructor provides you. FOLLOW THE DIRECTIONS, FOLLOW THE DIRECTIONS, FOLLOW THE DIRECTIONS! Generally, they will tell you what documentation style to use, which organizational pattern is preferred, and a host of other valuable information. Save yourself and your instructor a lot of headaches by paying careful attention to the instructions. If you receive no instructions, then ask the instructor what she or he prefers. No professor keeps that information secret, and most will be happy to help or refer you to places on campus where help is available.

If the documentation style of a paper is left up to you, you have three choices: MLA, APA, and the traditional notes-and-bibliography (Turabian) format.

MLA (MODERN LANGUAGE ASSOCIATION) STYLE

MLA style is an in-text documentation style used primarily in the humanities. It involves documenting sources in parenthetical references throughout the text of the paper. References in the text must clearly point to specific sources in the list of Works Cited, which follows the text of the research paper and lists in proper format all of the sources cited in the paper.

In-Text Documentation

The parenthetical reference in the body of your paper typically consists of the author's last name followed by the page number of the original work. If the author's name is used in the text of the paper, only the page number appears in the parenthetical reference. Look at the sample paragraph below.

```
One notable Dickinson critic sums up "The Soul selects her own Society" when
he writes, "... [This poem] is related to Emily Dickinson's choice of the life
of seclusion... preferring her own small circles and closing the door to the
general world" (Anderson 171). Anderson further explains that Dickinson's choice
was the result of some emotional crisis, the nature of which sparks endless
speculation (176).
```

Parenthetical references follow the cited information. They are usually placed at the end of a sentence before the punctuation or at some other natural break in a long, complex sentence. Quotations longer than four lines are indented ten spaces from the left margin. The parenthetical reference follows the last line before the punctuation. Quotation marks are not used.

```
Synaesthesia is the describing of something through one of your five senses
that is usually described through another of your five senses. Take for exam-
ple, the figure of speech, "The light exploded into the room." How can light,
something that you see, be described in terms of something you hear? (Carey 53)
```

If you cite more than one source written by the same author, the parenthetical reference must also include the title of the source. In these references, commas separate the elements.

```
The story begins innocently enough. "On Thanksgiving morning I'm still in my
nightgown thinking of Vic when Dad raps on my apartment door," but the conflict
becomes immediately apparent (Mukherjee, Orbiting, 4).
```

If you quote an indirect source—someone else's report of a conversation, interview, etc.—use the abbreviation *qtd.* in the note before the source.

```
Basil regarded his new daughter as "a gift from God, the very vision of per-
fection" (qtd. in Callanan 34).
```

The preceding information covers most of the situations you will encounter as you document, but not all of them. Be sure to consult a recent MLA style manual for details about citing other categories of sources, such as books with multiple authors, pamphlets, journals, and so on. Most bookstores and libraries have the *MLA Handbook for Writers of Research Papers.*

Works Cited

Follow the text of the paper with a *Works Cited* page, a complete listing of all sources cited in the paper. Don't include sources you haven't cited, even if they were an important part of your research. If you wish to list sources you haven't cited, include another page called *Works Consulted*.

Start the Works Cited page by placing the page number in the upper right-hand corner, one-half inch from the top of the page. Double-space and begin the listing. Sources are listed alphabetically by author, by title if there is no author. The first line of each entry begins flush with the left margin; subsequent lines are indented five spaces. Here is an example of part of a Works Cited page.

```
                              Works Cited

Anderson, Charles R. Emily Dickinson's Poetry: Stairway of Surprise. New York:
    Holt, Rinehart and Winston, 1960.
Cody, John. After Great Pain: The Inner life of Emily Dickinson. Cambridge, Mass-
    achusetts: Harvard UP, 1971.
DeManuel, Dolores. "A Certain Shaft of Light: Inner Illumination in Dickinson's
    Poems." Journal of 19th Century American Literature 8 (1995): 123-144.
Pickard, John B. Emily Dickinson: An Introduction and an Interpretation. New
    York: Barnes and Noble, 1967.
Underwood, Maureen. "Re-Evaluating Emily Dickinson." Springfield Times 18 Oct.
    1996, A6.
```

Consult an MLA style guide for a complete listing of Works Cited samples. Pay careful attention to how the information in each entry is organized and punctuated.

APA (AMERICAN PSYCHOLOGICAL ASSOCIATION) STYLE

The APA style of documentation is used primarily in the social sciences.

In-Text Documentation

Like the MLA format, the APA format involves documenting sources in parenthetical references throughout the text of the paper. The difference is that APA parenthetical references include the author's last name, the date of the publication, and sometimes the page number. Page numbers are always given for quotations; for paraphrases and summaries giving the page number or not is left up to the writer, though your instructor may ask you to include page numbers.

If the author's name is used in the text of the paper, the date of the source follows the author's name, and the page number, if any, comes at the end of the sentence. Look at the sample paragraph below. Notes in the text point to specific sources in the list of References, which follows the text of the research paper and lists in proper format all of the sources cited in the paper.

```
Alexander (1992) compiled completely different results when he conducted his
experiment. The only reported variation in experimental conditions was time of
day. Another attempt in 1994 by University of Michigan researchers to repeat
the experiment yielded even more variant results (Edison, 1994).
```

Be sure to consult a recent APA style manual for details about citing sources. Most bookstores and libraries have copies of the *Publication Manual of the American Psychological Association.*

References

Follow the paper and any notes and/or appendices with a page titled References. This page is numbered along with the rest of the paper. Center the title References one and one-half inches from the top of the page. Double-space and begin the first entry. All entries begin flush with the left margin. Subsequent lines are indented three spaces. Alphabetize the entries by the author's last name, by title if no author is listed. Once again, consult an APA style guide for a complete listing of References samples. Pay careful attention to how the information in each entry is organized and punctuated.

```
                              References

Camden, A. (1995). Suburban sprawl. New York: Harper.
Doing in the land. (1993, August). Atlantic, pp. 34-35.
Franke, G. (Ed.). (1989). History of urban geography. New York: Hayden.
Pidgeon, B. (1997, December 19). The land up for grabs. [Interview with Des
   Moines Register staff]. Des Moines Register, p. B3.
Sessions, R. (Producer & Director). (1992). Covering America [Documentary]. Los
   Angeles, CA: HBO.
U.S. Bureau of the Census. (1988). Interpretations of census data. Washington:
   Government Printing Office.
```

NOTE-AND-BIBLIOGRAPHY STYLE

Use the note-and-bibliography form of documentation only if you have been specifically instructed to use footnotes or endnotes rather than in-text documentation. In this style, documented material is followed by consecutive superscript numbers that correspond with bibliographic information in footnotes at the bottom of the page or notes at the end of the paper.

Notes

Endnotes and footnotes contain the information needed to locate the source of the information: author's name, title of the work, publication information, and page number(s). Endnotes go at the end of your text, before the bibliography, while footnotes go at the bottom of the page they refer to.

Number notes consecutively throughout the paper. Place superscript numbers (raised slightly above the line of type) at the end of the sentence containing the information. Indent the first line of each note (footnote or endnote) five spaces. Subsequent lines are flush with the left margin. Full bibliographic information is included only once. Additional notes from the same source contain only the author's name and the page number. If the second note from the same source comes immediately after the first, you can write just the abbreviation *ibid.* and the page number. The example below illustrates a footnote.

```
One notable Dickinson critic sums up "The Soul selects her own Society" when
he writes, "... [This poem] is related to Emily Dickinson's choice of the life
of seclusion... preferring her own small circles and closing the door to the
general world."[1] He further explains that Dickinson's choice was the result of
some emotional crisis, the nature of which sparks endless speculation.[2]


    [1] Charles R. Anderson, Emily Dickinson's Poetry: Stairway of Surprise (New
York: Holt, Rinehart and Winston, 1960) 171.


    [2] Ibid. 176.
```

Bibliography

Follow the paper and notes with a separate page titled Bibliography or Works Cited. Use the MLA format to construct this page unless your instructor tells you otherwise.

Skill Building Until Next Time

Choose a subject that requires a research paper. Go to the library and peruse a few issues of scholarly journals in that discipline. Choose three or four articles that interest you. Notice how the writers present their arguments and organize the evidence in support of the arguments. It may be a good idea to photocopy one of the shorter research-based articles, one with documentation similar to what you will be asked to use. That way you'll have a well-written sample on hand when you start your research.

L·E·S·S·O·N

HOW TO PREPARE FOR A TEST

23

LESSON SUMMARY

This lesson will show you a step-by-step process you can use to prepare for any upcoming test, whether it's an in-class essay test, a multiple-choice midterm, or a lengthy final exam. You'll find out how you can use the skills that you learned in this book to prepare for and improve your performance on all kinds of tests you'll take throughout your college career. First, you'll find a timeline to help you plan out a study schedule for your tests. Then, you'll learn several test strategies you can employ while actually taking a test, including how to use your writing skills to answer typical test questions in courses ranging from history to anthropology to literature.

Many students get nervous or anxious thinking about taking an upcoming test or final exam, so don't feel you're alone if you experience such feelings. The best way to combat test anxiety is to **be prepared.** You've probably heard that advice before but may not know exactly how to go about it.

This lesson will show you several ways to prepare for upcoming tests. The fact that you're reading this book gives you a distinct advantage because you've already increased your writing skills by completing the lessons in this book. Your improved writing skills will enable you to perform better on various tests that you take during your college career because instructors expect students to know basic grammar and organization skills. Especially when you're taking an essay test, these skills are vital to your success.

An important step in preparing for your tests is to be aware of when they will occur. With the hectic pace of college life, it can be easy to forget a test date. Therefore, it's best to write down all upcoming test dates on your calendar. That way, you won't be caught off guard. Once you've charted all your test dates in a calendar, you can set up a plan of preparation.

PREPARING FOR YOUR TEST STEP BY STEP

Several test preparation timelines are presented below. You can write each stage down on your calendar. These steps will work well for midterm and final exams, as well as for any other tests your instructor gives you at least three weeks' notice for. Of course, if you have an instructor who gives pop quizzes unannounced, then you need to be ready every day you have class. However, you usually will have at least three or four weeks' notice for upcoming exams. Indeed, most instructors will give you a *syllabus*, or course outline, at the beginning of the course with all the test dates clearly marked. Follow the steps below to confidently face your next test.

THREE OR FOUR WEEKS BEFORE THE TEST

Plan ahead. About a month before the test, take the following steps:

1. Ask your instructor to clarify what will be on the test. Take notes on whatever the instructor tells you and focus your review on those items that will be tested.

2. Review your notes from class lectures. Get copies of any notes you missed from other students or the instructor. Read your lecture notes and outline them in a concise form to get the most out of them.

3. Review all assigned textbook readings, paying special attention to any marginal notes or highlighting you did. Write down each chapter's main idea in the margin of the book or in your class notebook for later review.

4. Create flash cards to memorize key concepts, dates, or terms that you think will be on the test. Carry the flash cards with you so you can pull them out and study them whenever you have a few minutes of downtime. Before you create a flash card for an unfamiliar term in your assigned reading, try to determine the word's meaning from its context in the textbook before looking it up in a dictionary.

TWO WEEKS BEFORE THE TEST

Now is the time to get some more specific information about your test.

1. Ask your instructor how the test will be organized—true/false, multiple choice, fill-in-the-blank, short answer, essay, and so on.

2. Find out how much the test will affect your grade. If it's a final exam that is worth 50 percent of your grade, you'll want to spend more time studying for it than if it's a weekly test worth five percent of your grade. Check with your instructor or look at the syllabus (course outline) you received at the beginning of the term.

3. Pretend you're the instructor—what things would you ask for on this test? Make up a few sample questions and then write out your answers to them. This is particularly good practice for essay questions. You just might find those same questions on the test!

4. Jot down any questions you have about the material you're reviewing to ask the instructor. It's better to clarify your questions before the test than after.

ONE WEEK BEFORE THE TEST

During the week before the test, you should be intensifying your study so you won't have to cram the day before the exam.

1. Review your notes again and highlight the portions that you don't know yet. Then the next time you review, you won't have to re-read all the information that you already know; instead, you can focus on learning or memorizing the highlighted information.

2. Continue studying your flash cards of important terms, dates, and facts. Create more flash cards as needed.

3. Create lists, outlines, rhymes, or anything else that will help you remember the information you are studying.

4. Study with another student or group of students. A small group works better than a large one. Stay focused on the material and discuss concepts and possible test questions with each other.

TWO OR THREE DAYS BEFORE THE TEST

In the few days before the test, take care of your body as well as of your mind.

1. Continue your review. Since you started reviewing early, there is no need to cram at this point. Cramming may confuse you and take away your body's energy—and you'll need that energy on test day!

2. Do some physical activity to increase the oxygen flow to your brain. Don't wear yourself out trying to run a marathon, but moderate exercise will help your brain to achieve peak performance during the upcoming test. Brisk walking is an excellent energy-building exercise.

3. Eat a well-balanced diet so you won't get fatigued or become sick before you take the test. You'll want to be in good health so your brain will function clearly during the test. Don't fall prey to the cramming, coffee-drinking, no-sleep lifestyle that has become popular among some students right before test time. It's just not worth the damage to your health, and it could prevent you from doing well on the test.

4. Along with exercise and eating right, it's important to get enough sleep before the big day. You don't want to fall asleep while you're in the middle of writing a great answer to an essay question only to find that you don't have time to finish it once you awaken.

THE DAY OF THE TEST

Here are some tips to help you do well on test day:

1. Allow extra time to get to class or the examining room early, so you don't have to rush. If you miss an important announcement at the beginning of class, it could hurt your score.

2. Ensure that you have all the materials needed for the test. If you are allowed to bring a textbook, dictionary, or other reference to the test, by all means do so. You may need scratch paper to write on during the test. Bring extra pens or pencils too.

3. Listen carefully to all of the announcements and directions given by the instructor before you begin the test. Even if the test is in front of you, don't become so distracted by it that you don't hear what the instructor is saying. Sometimes instructors override what is written on the test itself or will tell you to write in a change on the test.

4. Look quickly through the entire test to see how many questions are asked. Be sure you know how much time you have for taking the test and read all written instructions carefully. Take a moment to jot down an estimate of how much time you can spend on each portion or question on the test. If three essay questions are asked and you have 60 minutes to complete the test, then you can spend 20 minutes on each one. Of that time, you should plan to spend about half on thinking about your answer and half on actually writing it.

STRATEGIES TO USE DURING THE TEST

Once you've read the directions carefully, looked briefly over the entire test, and mentally noted the amount of time you have to complete the test, you can begin taking the test with confidence. Here are several strategies that you can use while you are actually taking the test to increase your chances of getting a good score. They include managing emotional issues, using your time wisely, avoiding errors, using your writing skills to ace tough questions, knowing tips on how to get the right answers for different kinds of questions, and checking your work if you finish early.

MANAGING EMOTIONAL ISSUES

Take the Test One Question at a Time

Focus all of your attention on the one question you're answering. Block out any thoughts about questions you've already finished or concerns about what's coming next. Concentrate your thinking where it will do the most good—on the question you're answering now.

Develop a Positive Attitude

Keep reminding yourself that you're prepared. In fact, if you've completed the lessons in this book, you're probably better prepared than many others who are taking the test. Remember, it's only a test, and you're going to do your **best**. That's all anyone can ask of you. If that nagging drill sergeant voice inside your head starts sending negative messages, combat them with positive ones of your own. Tell yourself:

- "I'm doing just fine."
- "I've prepared for this test."
- "I know exactly what to do."
- "I know I can get the score I'm shooting for."

You get the idea. Remember to drown out negative messages with positive ones of your own.

If You Lose Your Concentration

Don't worry about it! It's normal. During a long test it happens to everyone. When your mind is stressed or overexerted, it takes a break whether you want it to or not. It's easy to get your concentration back if you simply acknowledge the fact that you've lost it and take a quick break. You brain needs very little time (seconds, really) to rest.

Put your pencil down and close your eyes. Take a deep breath, hold it for a moment, and let it out slowly. Listen to the sound of your breathing as you repeat this two more times. The few seconds that this takes is really all the time your brain needs to relax and get ready to focus again. This exercise also helps you control your heart rate, so that you can keep anxiety at bay.

Try this technique several times in the days before the test when you feel stressed. The more you practice, the better it will work for you on the day of the test.

If You Freeze

Don't worry about a question that stumps you even though you're sure you know the answer. Mark it and go on to the next question. You can come back to the "stumper" later. Try to put it out of your mind completely until you come back to it. Just let your subconscious mind chew on the question while your conscious mind focuses on the other questions (one at a time—of course). Chances are, the memory block will be gone by the time you return to the question.

If you freeze before you ever begin the test, here's what to do:

1. Do some deep breathing to help yourself relax and focus.
2. Remind yourself that you're prepared.
3. Take a little time to look over the test.
4. Read a few of the questions.
5. Decide which ones are the easiest and start there.

Before long, you'll be "in the groove."

TIME STRATEGIES

One of the most important—and nerve-wracking—elements of taking a test is time. You'll only be allowed a certain amount of time to complete the test, so it's important to use every minute wisely.

Pace Yourself

The most important time strategy is **pacing yourself.** Before you begin, take just a few seconds to survey the test, making note of the number of questions and of the sections that look easier than the rest. Then, make a rough time schedule based on the amount of time available to you.

Keep Moving

Once you begin the test, **keep moving.** If you work slowly in an attempt to make fewer mistakes, your mind will become bored and begin to wander. You'll end up making far more mistakes if you're not concentrating. Worse, if you take too long to answer questions that stump you, you may end up running out of time before you finish.

So don't stop for difficult questions. Skip them and move on. You can come back to them later if you have time. Answering the easier questions first helps to build your confidence and gets you in the testing groove. Who knows? As you go through the test, you may even stumble across some relevant information to help you answer those tough questions.

Don't Rush

Keep moving, but **don't rush.** Think of your mind as a seesaw. On one side is your emotional energy. On the other side is your intellectual energy. When your emotional energy is high, your intellectual capacity is low. Remember how difficult it is to reason with someone when you're angry? On the other hand, when your intellectual energy is high, your emotional energy is low. Rushing raises your emotional energy and reduces your intellectual capacity. Move quickly to keep your mind from wandering, but don't rush and get yourself flustered.

Check Yourself

Check yourself at the halfway mark. If you're a little ahead, you know you're on track and may even have a little time left to check your work. If you're a little behind, you have several choices. You can pick up the pace a little, but do this *only* if you can do it comfortably. Remember—**don't rush!** You can also skip around in the remaining portion of the test to pick up as many easy points as possible. This strategy has one drawback, however. If you are marking a bubble-style answer sheet, and you put the right answers in the wrong bubbles—they're wrong. So pay close attention to the question numbers if you decide to do this.

AVOIDING ERRORS

When you take the test, you want to make as few errors as possible in the questions you answer. Here are a few tactics to keep in mind.

Control Yourself

Remember that comparison between your mind and a seesaw? Keeping your emotional energy low and your intellectual energy high is the best way to avoid mistakes. If you feel stressed or worried, stop for a few seconds. Acknowledge the feeling (Hmmm! I'm feeling a little pressure here!), take a few deep breaths, and send yourself a few positive messages. This relieves your emotional anxiety and boosts your intellectual capacity.

Answers

This may seem like a silly warning, but it is important. Place your answers in the right blanks or the corresponding ovals on the answer sheet if your instructor uses an electronically scored test. Right answers in the wrong place earn no points. It's a good idea to check every five to ten questions to make sure you're in the right spot. That way you won't need much time to correct your answer sheet if you have made an error.

If you are writing your answers on the test itself or a separate sheet of paper, be sure to write neatly and clearly. You could get points taken off if the instructor can't read your handwriting.

USING YOUR WRITING SKILLS

Your polished writing skills will enable you to perform better on a wide variety of tests. Here are several writing skills that you learned in this book that you can use to ace tough test questions. Typical examples of the types of test questions you can expect from beginning college courses and the writing skills you can use to master them are discussed below.

Proper Punctuation and Capitalization

The punctuation skills you learned in this book will help you to do well on several different types of tests, most notably on essay and short-answer tests. For instance, if you're taking a test in a psychology course and you're asked to discuss the work of Carl Jung in a short answer, you'll be in trouble if you forget the rule about commas and nonrestrictive clauses and write something like this: "Carl Jung was not a psychologist, who agreed with Freud." If you're unsure why this statement is false, now would be a good time to review Lesson 4.

In addition to punctuation rules, you'll also need to employ the capitalization rules you gained from this book to do well on short-answer and essay tests. Suppose you're taking a test in a history course, and you're asked to describe the League of Nations. You'll probably get points taken off if you write this: "The League of nations existed from, 1920 to 1946 when the League passed on it's heritage to the united Nations." Even though the facts are correct in this statement, several capitalization and punctuation rules have been broken. Can you identify all of the errors? If not, review Lessons 1, 4, 5, and 7. You'll see that the correct way to write the above statement is this: "The League of Nations existed from 1920 to 1946, when the league passed on its heritage to the United Nations."

Correct Use of Pronouns

Now that you know how to use pronouns correctly in writing tasks, you won't upset your instructors by using the wrong pronoun in the wrong place. Since pronouns are so often misused in spoken English, they offer a challenge to conscientious writers who don't want to annoy their instructors by making common pronoun mistakes. A test in Economics 101 might ask a question like this: "Contrast capitalism and communism." Your instructor will be annoyed if you write, "Their both forms of economic systems, and they're policies differ greatly according to there beliefs." Don't you agree that this sentence is confusing? Although it is an extreme example, it shows the need for students to know how to use pronouns. If you have trouble with any pronouns, review Lessons 13 and 14. Create flash cards with sample sentences using each pronoun that gives you difficulty and study the cards for a few weeks.

Using Diction Wisely

Your skills in eliminating wordiness, using the active voice, and avoiding emotionally loaded language will serve you well on many short-answer and essay tests. Another aspect of diction you learned about in this book is using gender-neutral language. If you're taking an essay test in a women's studies course, you definitely wouldn't want to fill your answer with terms such as *mankind, businessman*, or *poetess*, or use the words *girls* or *the weaker sex* to describe women!

GETTING THE RIGHT ANSWERS

Make sure you understand what the question is asking before you answer it. If you're not sure of what's being asked, you'll never know whether you're giving the right answer. You can use the tips given below to help you select the right answers for multiple-choice, true/false, fill-in-the-blank, and essay questions. Since these questions are so different from each other, helpful hints for getting the right answers are given for each type.

Multiple-Choice Questions

For multiple-choice questions, if the answer isn't readily apparent, look for clues in the answer choices. Notice the similarities and differences in the answer choices. Sometimes this helps to put the question in a new perspective and makes it easier to answer. If you're still not sure of the answer, use the process of elimination. First, eliminate any answer choices that are obviously wrong. Then reason your way through the remaining choices. You may be able to use relevant information from other parts of the test. If you can't eliminate any of the answer choices, you might be better off to skip the question and come back to it later. If you can't eliminate any answer choices to improve your odds when you come back later, then make a guess and move on.

True/False Questions

If the question is a true/false question, read the entire statement before deciding if it's true or false. For a statement to be true, the entire statement must be true. Often, the first part of a statement will be true, but the second part will be false. Use the reading skill of distinguishing between fact and opinion for help in answering these questions. Look for words that signal extremes, such as *never, always, everyone, all,* or *none.* Statements with these words in them are often false just because they include these extreme words.

Fill-In-the-Blank Questions

If the question is a fill-in-the-blank one, remember to look closely at the question for clues to the answer. For example, is the word before the blank *a* or *an*? If so, you'll know whether the word you need to fill in the blank should begin with a vowel or a consonant. You can also look at the length of the blank line since it might tell you if the answer you are to write in is long or short. As long as your instructor doesn't take points away for guessing, you might as well take your best guess on these questions. Think back to the flash cards you made or the lists of terms specific to the test's subject and insert one of those words that seem applicable.

Essay Questions

If you're answering an essay question, it's very important to read and re-read the question very carefully before you plunge into answering it. If you misread what the question is asking, you could waste valuable time and points by answering the wrong question.

Several key words are often used in essay questions, so you'll have a head start if you know what they mean before the test. If you are unsure of the meaning of any of the following words, look those words up in a dictionary and memorize their meanings before taking an essay test.

Compare	Describe	List
Contrast	Discuss	Outline
Criticize	Evaluate	Prove
Define	Interpret	Review

After you read the question very carefully and know what it is asking, jot down an outline or at least a list of items you plan to include in your answer before you begin writing. In fact, you should usually spend about half of the time you have for your essay question simply planning what you're going to write. Taking time to organize your answer before you begin can increase your score dramatically and can also eliminate the need for scribbling out sentences and trying to squeeze in extra facts you forgot the first time. Spend more time creating strong topic sentences for each paragraph than randomly writing down all the details you can remember about the topic. Using these tips will help you to perform better on the next essay test you encounter.

Review the punctuation, capitalization, and grammar rules in this book before taking any essay tests. In addition to using correct grammar and punctuation, you may also impress your instructor with other writing skills discussed in this book, such as using strong verbs to indicate action, avoiding emotionally loaded language, and maintaining a consistent point of view.

Another writing skill you learned in this book is how to develop ideas, which should increase the quality of your essay answers. If you've forgotten any of these things, refer back to the applicable lesson for a review. By using your new writing skills, you'll be able to perform better on the next essay test you take, no matter what the subject of the course is.

IF YOU FINISH EARLY

Use any time you have left at the end of the test to check your work. First, make certain you've put the answers in the right places, especially if you're marking a bubble-style answer sheet. Also, make sure you've answered each question only once. Questions with more than one answer are usually marked wrong. If you've erased an answer, make sure you've done a good job. Check for stray marks on your answer sheet that could distort your score.

After you've checked for these easy errors, take a second look at the more difficult questions. You've probably heard the folk wisdom about never changing an answer. It's not always good advice. If you have a good reason for thinking a response is wrong, change it.

If you're taking an essay test, look back over your answers and take the time to correct any spelling errors or to add words you may have forgotten to write in the first time. It's easy to miss writing the words *the* or *an* when you're writing quickly. If you need to make a small correction, neatly cross out the word and carefully write your correction above it. Instructors don't like to read messy essay answers that are full of cross-outs and scribbles, so be as neat as you can when changing or adding words to your answer.

AFTER THE TEST

Once you've finished, *congratulate yourself.* You've worked hard to prepare; now it's time to enjoy yourself and relax. Plan a celebration or treat yourself to a fancy dinner or a new sweater. You deserve it after all your hard work.

Skill Building One Last Time

Choose one upcoming test that you have to study for and write down a study plan for it using the timeline given in this lesson. Jot down specific steps you'll take to prepare for the test, such as re-reading chapters 2–6 in the assigned textbook, asking the instructor to review the principles listed in chapter 4 that you weren't sure of, or reviewing one or more of the lessons in this book. After you complete this exercise, carry the study plan with you, so you can remember to complete each step as your test date draws near.